AI in Energy: Powering the Smart Grid

GoodMan, Volume 1

Patrick Mukosha

Published by Patrick Mukosha, 2025.

AI in Energy: Powering the Smart Grid

Optimizing Power Generation, Grid Distribution, Energy Consumption, and Renewable Forecasting.

Copyright Notice

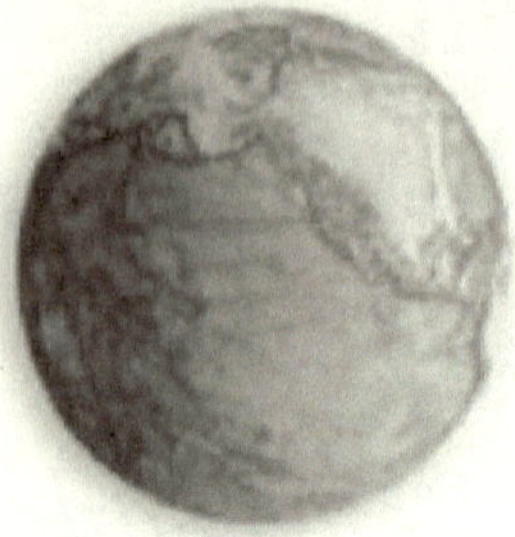

First published: August, 2025

Publisher: Dr Patrick Chisenga Mukosha

Trademarks

All terms mentioned in this book that are known to be trademarks or service marks have been appropriately capitalized. The Author and the publisher cannot attest to the accuracy of this information. Use of a term in this book should not be regarded as affecting the validity of any trademark or service mark.

Warning and Disclaimer

Every effort has been made to make this book as complete and as accurate as possible, but no warranty or fitness is implied. The information provided in this book is on as is basis. The Author and the Publisher shall have neither liability nor responsibility to any person or entity with respect to any loss or damage arising from the use the information contained in this book.

Author: Patrick Chisenga Mukosha PhD

Abstract

The world's energy situation is changing dramatically, moving away from reliance on fossil fuels and toward digital intelligence. *From smart grids to renewable integration, artificial intelligence is changing the way the world produces, distributes, and uses energy.* This is seen in AI in Energy.

It *examines how machine learning, predictive analytics, and intelligent automation are transforming energy systems by improving grid dependability, anticipating renewable production, optimizing power generation, and promoting sustainability on a large scale.* It was written by a well-known technologist and energy strategist.

This book deconstructs the energy of the future into practical ideas and applications:

- **Smart Grids:** How digital twins, edge computing, and AI-powered sensors build adaptable, self-healing energy networks.
- **Power Generation Optimization**: Increasing productivity, decreasing downtime, and dynamically balancing load through the use of predictive analytics.
- **Grid Distribution:** Using demand response, fault detection, and microgrid intelligence driven by AI, energy distribution is being reinvented.
- **Energy Consumption:** AI-enabled energy management solutions allow for the personalization of efficiency at the domestic, business, and national levels.
- **Renewable Forecasting:** Using deep learning to forecast hydro, wind, and solar output with previously unheard-of accuracy.

By demonstrating how data, algorithms, and human creativity can come together to create the next-generation energy ecosystem—one that is cleaner, smarter, and self-optimizing—AI in energy bridges the gap between engineering and intelligence.

This *book offers the road map for comprehending how AI is driving the energy revolution, one intelligent watt at a time, regardless of your background as an energy executive, data scientist, legislator, or entrepreneur.*

Dr. John H. Cunningham – Energy & Utilities Consultant

Chapter 1: The Grid's Development: From Wires to Intelligence

1.1. From Edison's Light Bulb to the Lifeblood of the World

The first central power plant in history, the *Pearl Street Station in New York City*, was turned on *by Thomas Edison in 1882*. Powering a few hundred lamps throughout lower Manhattan, it provided *Direct Current* (DC) electricity to just 59 consumers. The electric age began at this time. Soon after, George Westinghouse and Nikola Tesla promoted *Alternating Current* (AC), which made it possible for electricity to traverse great distances. More than just a technological competition, the AC vs. DC "*War of Currents*" established the groundwork for the centralized power systems that still rule today.

Grids grew into enormous, linked networks throughout the course of the following century. Power from massive coal facilities, hydroelectric dams, and subsequently nuclear power plants was sent into homes and factories via transmission lines. With its ability to drive urbanization, industrial revolutions, and digital change, electricity became the lifeblood of modern society. A one-way power flow from centralized producers to passive consumers, however, was the mainstay of the system.

1.1.1. The Problems with Conventional Grids

Although they supported economic expansion, older grids were not designed to meet the demands of the modern world. Their shortcomings are becoming more obvious:

1.1.1.1. **Rigidity**

Strict supply-demand balancing governs how traditional grids function. In order to prevent shortages, operators frequently overproduce, wasting resources and causing inefficiencies. For instance, billions of dollars are spent on infrastructure to manage the infrequent surges in demand that only happen a few hours a year in the United States.

- **Example:** Rolling blackouts during the 2020 heatwaves in California demonstrated the grid's inability to swiftly adjust to unexpected spikes in demand while renewable output decreased at sunset (the so-called "duck curve" issue).

1.1.1.2. **Inefficiency**

Approximately 8% of the electricity produced worldwide is lost in the transmission and distribution process. Power plants themselves are inefficient; only 30–40% of fuel is converted into useful power by thermal plants, with the remaining fuel being wasted as heat.

- **India Case Study**: India's traditional grid loses an estimated 20% of electricity in transmission and distribution, while having one of the fastest-growing energy markets. This is mostly because of theft and aging equipment. Frequent outages and increased expenditures are caused by this inefficiency.

1.1.1.3. **Vulnerability**

Conventional grids are centralized and vulnerable to interruptions from equipment malfunctions, hacking, and natural disasters. Entire regions can be affected by a single fault.

- **Case Study: The 2003 Northeast Blackout (United States & Canada):**

An Ohio utility's control room failed to detect a software flaw. Fifty million people in eight U.S. states and Ontario lost power in a matter of hours. An estimated $6 billion was lost as a result of the paralysis of communications, hospitals, and transportation.

- **Case Study: Ukraine, 2015:**

230,000 citizens lost power when hackers breached the nation's electrical grid. This demonstrated the vulnerability of centralized systems as it was the first known cyberattack to successfully take down a power infrastructure.

1.1.2. Why Intelligent, Adaptive, and Autonomous Systems Are Necessary for the Future

With the ability to anticipate, prepare, and comprehend their environments, autonomous systems can complete tasks, reach objectives, and engage with their environment with little assistance from humans. AI's position in autonomous systems is essential to transforming how we interact with the real and virtual worlds.

By combining deep learning and neural networks, autonomous AI optimizes operations in a variety of industries by automating complicated processes, handling real-time data processing, making quick judgments, and adapting to changing situations.

In the past, the electric grid was built for a more straightforward scenario in which a few sizable power plants produced electricity that travelled in a single path to homes and businesses. However, the grid now has to deal with issues that its initial designers did not foresee. Three strong forces—decentralization, decarbonisation, and digitization—define the energy landscape of the twenty-first century. Collectively, they call for a smart grid that is also flexible and self-sufficient.

1.1.3. Important ITS NLP Functions:

1.1.3.1. Consumers to Prosumers: Decentralization

The conventional "hub-and-spoke" grid is disintegrating. Nowadays, millions of residences and commercial buildings generate their own energy using biogas systems, tiny wind turbines, and rooftop solar panels.

They are now prosumers—*simultaneously producing, storing, and consuming electricity*—instead of passive consumers thanks to battery storage and electric vehicles (EVs).

In order to maintain stability and control two-way power flows, this decentralization calls for real-time intelligence.

- **Example: Germany's Energiewende**: In Germany, individuals, farms, and cooperatives own about 50% of the renewable capacity rather than utilities. Without sophisticated digital tools that forecast, balance, and dispatch energy in milliseconds, it would be difficult to manage this patchwork of producers.
  Decentralized networks would collapse into chaos in the absence of intelligent systems.

1.1.3.2. The Challenge of Renewable Integration in Decarbonisation

Renewable energy usage is accelerating due to the global drive to achieve net-zero emissions. However, solar and wind are erratic and variable by nature. Even though the sun and wind don't always shine and blow, society nonetheless requires electricity all the time. Conventional grids overproduce and waste energy to deal with variability. The grid of the future must anticipate and adjust to it.

- **Google DeepMind & Wind Energy Case Study:** Google used artificial intelligence (AI) on its wind farms in the Midwest of the United States to predict output 36 hours ahead of time. This increased wind energy's economic value by 20% and made it a more dependable resource. Renewable energy sources become grid assets rather than liabilities thanks to this predictive knowledge.

Only AI-driven, adaptive forecasting and balancing systems can remain reliable as the proportion of renewable energy sources increases without using fossil fuel backup.

1.1.4. Digitization: Converting Information into Choices

Data is everywhere on the modern grid: sensors embedded in power lines and substations, smart meters, IoT-enabled gadgets, and weather satellites. Petabytes of data can be produced annually by a single utility.

However, without intelligence, data is meaningless. This volume is too large for traditional systems to handle, and they cannot respond fast enough to stop cascade failures. Real-time operation optimization, failure prediction, and anomaly detection are made possible by AI and machine learning.

Example: Consider **Enel in Italy**, which converted its whole grid into a digital ecosystem by installing 33 million smart meters. These days, AI systems can automatically reroute electricity during outages, identify theft, and balance demand—all of which minimize downtime and save millions of dollars in lost revenue.

The grid is now more observable thanks to digitization, and AI makes it actionable.

1.1.5. The Argument in Favour of Autonomy

The grid will become too complicated for human operators to handle alone in the ensuing decades. Decision-making needs to happen instantly because of the millions of dispersed assets, real-time volatility, and cyber threats.

Self-healing, self-optimizing, and self-defending autonomous systems are necessary, not optional:

a. *An AI-powered grid can autonomously cut off endangered transmission lines, redirect electricity, and manage storage systems during wildfires, saving lives and averting cascading disasters.*
b. *AI anomaly detection can isolate vulnerable nodes during cyberattacks while maintaining grid functionality.*

1.2. An Intelligent Grid That Functions Like a Nervous System

The grid of the future will function less like a mechanical device and more like a computerized nervous system. *In milliseconds, it will perceive, analyse, and react, anticipating issues before they arise, adjusting to unexpected disturbances, and picking up on historical trends.*

Autonomous, intelligent, and flexible systems are necessities. They serve as the cornerstone of the energy system of the future, one that must provide inexpensive, dependable, and clean power in the face of changing threats, growing demand, and climate change.

For this reason, *AI is the primary enabler of the energy revolution of the twenty-first century rather than only a tool.*

1.3. Decarbonisation through the Use of Renewable Energy

1.3.1. Overview: Fossil Fuels to the Grid of the Future

Coal, oil, and natural gas—*fuels that propelled industrial revolutions, illuminated cities, and stimulated economic growth*—were the foundation of the world's energy systems. They did, however, come at a high cost: *carbon emissions, which have dangerously hastened climate change.*

Decarbonisation is now our century's defining mission, not just a trendy term. The incorporation of renewable energy into national and international power grids is fundamental to this change.

1.3.2. The Drive for Integration of Renewable Energy

Three main factors are driving the need to decarbonize: technological innovation, economic competitiveness, and climate commitments:

- **Climate Commitments:** Over 140 nations have committed to achieving net-zero emissions by 2050 or before. Rapidly switching from fossil fuels to renewable energy sources is necessary for this.
- **Economic Competitiveness:** Solar and wind energy are already more affordable than coal and gas for new electricity generation in many regions of the world.
- **Technological Innovation**: Renewable energy sources are becoming more dependable and simpler to incorporate thanks to developments in energy storage, grid digitization,

and AI-driven forecasting.

In addition to substituting clean fuels for dirty ones, the energy transition aims to create a more intelligent and robust system that can support tomorrow's smart cities, electric cars, and digital economy.

1.4. The Difficulties of Renewable Energy Integration

Despite their abundance, renewables are difficult to integrate:

- **Intermittency:** On calm days, wind turbines remain motionless, while solar panels do not produce electricity at night. In the absence of adequate backup, this may result in energy shortages.

- **Grid Stability:** Millions of dispersed solar rooftops consuming electricity simultaneously were not the target of traditional systems, which were built for reliable, centralized power plants.
- **Storage Restrictions:** Even if lithium-ion batteries are becoming more affordable, it is still costly to store electricity on a national scale.
- **Infrastructure Gaps:** The transmission networks necessary to transport renewable electricity from windy coasts or sunny deserts to urban areas are lacking in many developing countries.

Although these obstacles are genuine, they can be overcome.

1.4.1. Ways to Integrate Effectively

To guarantee that renewables integrate smoothly into the grid, nations all around the world are experimenting with creative methods:

- **Smart Grids:** AI-enabled digital grids that are capable of instantly balancing supply and demand.

- **Energy Storage:** Large-scale storage is emerging as a key component of renewable integration, as evidenced by Tesla's massive battery farms in Australia and pumped-hydro storage in Switzerland.
- **Hybrid Systems:** To guarantee a steady supply, combine solar and wind power with nuclear, natural gas, or hydrogen.

Microgrids are localized networks that include storage and renewable energy sources; they are especially helpful in isolated or disaster-prone areas. Digital twins are virtual grid models that forecast the behaviour of new renewable energy sources prior to their actual installation.

1.5. Case Studies from the Real World

1.5.1. The Energiewende in Germany

Germany is now a global leader in solar and wind thanks to its audacious strategy to phase out nuclear and fossil fuels in favour of renewables. Nonetheless, the nation has had to deal with intermittency and the requirement for new transmission lines, which have taught it to be both ambitious and cautious.

1.5.2. Geothermal Powerhouse: Kenya

By utilizing its abundant geothermal resources in the Rift Valley, Kenya has emerged as a leader in renewable energy. Geothermal energy now accounts for about half of its electricity, offering a dependable and carbon-free base load.

1.5.3. The Rooftop Revolution in Australia

Nowadays, rooftop solar panels are installed in over 30% of Australian homes. Some of the most sophisticated grid-balancing solutions in the world have been developed as a result of the nation's difficulty shifting from adoption to integration.

1.5.4. China: Reaching Unprecedented Heights of Growth

More wind and solar power is being installed in China than in the entire world. Through its investments in ultra-high-voltage transmission lines, clean electricity from distant deserts and plateaus may reach cities across thousands of kilometres.

1.6. The Benefit of AI

The hidden weapon of renewable integration is turning out to be artificial intelligence:

- **Forecasting:** AI algorithms can accurately forecast solar and wind output minute by minute, lowering the likelihood of unexpected outages.
- **Optimization:** Like an orchestra conductor controlling many instruments, AI algorithms balance dispersed resources, including as storage, wind farms, and solar rooftops.
- **Predictive maintenance** lowers expenses and downtime by using sensors and artificial intelligence to identify early indications of turbine and panel wear.
- **Empowerment of the Consumer:** AI-powered applications enable homes to maximize their energy consumption by reselling excess electricity to the grid during periods of high demand.

1.7. The Path Ahead: Moving Toward a Grid Free of Carbon

A completely decarbonized energy system is the ideal scenario. Many countries intend to use storage, carbon-neutral technologies, and renewable energy sources to power their systems exclusively by 2035–2050.

New ideas include:

- **Virtual Power Plants:** Digital systems known as *Virtual Power Plants* (VPPs) connect thousands of tiny renewable energy providers into a single, adaptable grid.
- **Sector Coupling**: Combining industry, transportation, and heating with electricity to optimize the use of renewable resources.
- **Carbon-Negative Solutions**: These include technologies that actively take carbon from the atmosphere in addition to removing emissions, such as *Bioenergy with Carbon Capture* (BECCS).

1.7.1. A New Era of Energy

Rethinking how societies produce, distribute, and use energy is the goal of decarbonisation, which goes beyond only reducing carbon emissions. This period will be defined by the incorporation of renewable energy sources, which will change grids from inflexible wire networks into intelligent, flexible ecosystems. Whether or not the world can integrate renewables is no longer the question; rather, it is how swiftly and boldly we are prepared to take action.

1.8. Digitization: Data-Driven Energy

Due to the unparalleled visibility, control, and optimization of energy systems made possible by digitalization, the energy sector is undergoing a significant revolution. The goal of data-driven energy is to transform vast amounts of information into useful insight that improves sustainability, dependability, and efficiency.

1.8.1. Digital Energy Systems' Ascent

Reactive problem-solving, planned maintenance, and manual monitoring were key components of traditional electricity systems. The energy industry is transitioning to a proactive, predictive paradigm with the introduction of digital technologies, such as cloud computing, IoT sensors, and smart meters.

- **Smart Meters**: These gadgets give utilities dynamic load balancing by providing real-time usage data from millions of homes.
- **IoT Sensors in Power Plants:** By continuously monitoring transmission lines, boilers, and turbines, abnormalities can be found before they cause breakdowns.
- **Digital Twins:** By simulating real-world processes, virtual versions of energy assets allow for scenario planning and predictive maintenance.

Case Study: The Enel Group

The multinational energy corporation Enel Group optimizes maintenance schedules and cuts downtime by more than 20% by using digital twins of its power facilities to forecast equipment breakdowns.

1.8.2. Energy AI and Data Analytics

Advanced analytics and artificial intelligence transform unstructured data into insightful knowledge:

- **Load Forecasting**: To cut waste and avoid blackouts, machine learning algorithms forecast energy demand hours, days, or even weeks in advance.
- **Renewable Integration**: Grid operators can balance sporadic renewable sources with conventional energy by using AI to forecast variations in solar and wind power.
- **Energy Theft Detection**: Algorithms examine usage trends to spot anomalous activities, which helps cut down on distribution losses of electricity.
- **Example:** To increase safety and grid dependability during wildfire seasons, Pacific Gas & Electric (PG&E) in California employs AI to predict increases in electricity consumption.

1.8.3. Real-Time Energy Insights via Cloud and Edge Computing

Computing infrastructure that can process large data streams in real time is necessary for digitization:

- **Edge Computing**: By processing data close to its source, edge computing lowers latency and facilitates quicker decision-making. For example, in the event of a local fault, a substation can redirect power on its own.
- **Cloud platforms**: Combine information from thousands of sources to provide long-term trend tracking and centralized

analysis.

- **Example**: To increase operational efficiency by up to 15%, Siemens Smart Grid Solutions, for instance, uses cloud computing to give operators predictive data for grid optimization.

1.8.4. **Cybersecurity in Data-Driven Energy**

New vulnerabilities are introduced by cybersecurity in data-driven energy digitization. Energy infrastructure protection is crucial

- **Threat Detection:** AI keeps an eye on network activity to look for indications of cyberattacks.
- **Secure Communication:** Data integrity from smart meters to control centres is guaranteed by encryption.
- **Preventive measures** are guided by digital simulations that predict possible cyber-physical threats.
- **Case Study:** To safeguard vital energy infrastructure throughout the globe, ABB's cybersecurity frameworks incorporate AI-driven anomaly detection.

1.9. Advantages of an Energy Ecosystem Driven by Data

- **Operational Efficiency:** Better scheduling of power generation and distribution is made possible by real-time data.
- **Cost Savings:** Predictive maintenance lowers repair expenses and unscheduled outages.
- **Sustainability**: Carbon emissions are decreased through optimal integration of renewable energy sources.
- **Empowerment of the Customer**: Apps and smart meters let users keep an eye on and control how much energy they use.

1.9.1. The Path Ahead

Digitization is only the first step.

- Energy management systems that are completely autonomous will be a part of the future energy ecology.
- Predictive energy markets powered by AI.
- Peer-to-peer energy trading via blockchain technology.
- Grids with millions of intelligent devices that are seamlessly integrated.

Diagram: Digitisation – Data-Driven Energy

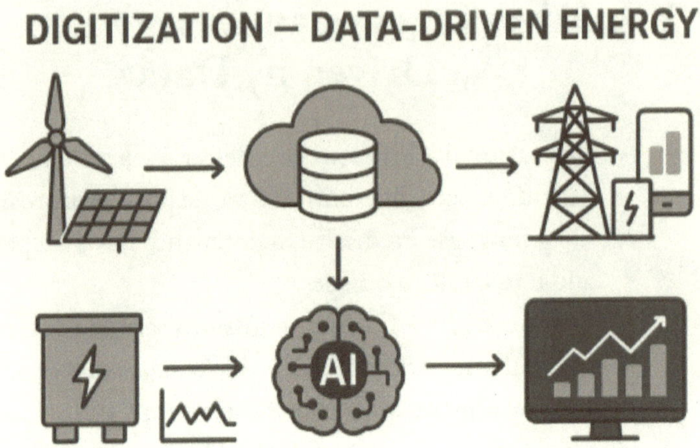

Figure 1: Digitisation – Data-Driven Energy

In conclusion, data is the energy sector's new fuel. Energy providers may build intelligent, adaptable, and resilient grids by utilizing machine learning, the Internet of Things, cloud computing, and edge computing. This change is based on digitization, which transforms energy from a commodity into a dynamic ecosystem that is driven by data.

1.10. The Way Forward: From Wires to Intelligence

When the electric grid first started off, it was just a few wires connecting a few lamps to a central generator. *It powered homes, communities, and businesses for more than a century, acting as the unseen backbone of development.* However, neither Tesla nor Edison could have predicted the demands made on this system today.

As we move into a new era, the grid will need to do much more than just carry electrons. *It needs to be able to sense, think, and adjust instantly.* The grid of the future will be a dynamic, interactive network rather than a rigid, one-way power flow. It will integrate intermittent renewable energy sources, balance millions of dispersed resources, and defend itself against threats ranging from cyberattacks to natural disasters.

This change is revolutionary rather than gradual. With artificial intelligence (AI) acting as its brain, the grid is changing from a passive infrastructure to an active intelligence system. *The grid is evolving toward self-healing and self-optimizing capabilities with digital twins simulating entire networks, autonomous control systems preventing blackouts, and machine learning forecasting patterns of renewable energy.*

The way forward is obvious: if the grid of the 20th century focused on scale, the grid of the 21st century is more concerned with intelligence. From control rooms to cloud platforms, from copper wires to neural networks, we are seeing the emergence of the AI-powered smart grid, a system that will not only satisfy the needs of contemporary life but also assist humanity in overcoming its biggest obstacle: creating a sustainable, carbon-neutral future.

The grid of the future will be able to think, anticipate, and adjust in addition to moving electrons. It will detect imbalances, reroute electricity, and potentially stop blackouts before they happen, much like a computerized nervous system. *AI will be at the heart of everything, allowing for a smart grid that is robust, adaptive, and self-healing.*

Edison's time of steam turbines and copper cables is giving way to an era of self-sufficient energy ecosystems, where artificial intelligence (AI) guarantees resilience, sustainability, and efficiency. This evolution is existential rather than merely technological. Rethinking the grid as an intelligent, living system is critical to the future of energy, climatic stability, and economic growth.

We shall examine where this intelligence starts—inside the core of electricity generation—as we move into Chapter 2.

1.10.1. **Important Takeaways and Insights**

1.10.1.1. **Historical Foundations Matter:**

- The grid started off as a centralized, one-way system, which influenced how civilizations developed but is now out of date, from Edison's Pearl Street Station (1882) to Tesla's AC revolution.

1.10.1.2. **Conventional Grids Are Becoming Less Sufficient:**

- **Rigidity:** The inability to adjust flexibly to changing demand, which results in blackouts (as in California 2020).
- **Inefficiency**: India loses up to 20% due to high transmission losses and waste.
- **Vulnerability:** As demonstrated by the Northeast Blackout of 2003 and the 2015 cyberattack on Ukraine, centralized control renders grids brittle.

1.10.1.3. **Change-Driven Megatrends**:

- **Decentralization**: According to Germany's Energiewende, consumers are now prosumers who produce their own energy.

- **Decarbonisation:** Renewable energy sources require real-time balancing and sophisticated forecasting (e.g., Google DeepMind's 20% increase in wind energy value).
- **Digitization**: AI-driven optimization is made possible by data from smart meters and Internet of Things sensors (e.g., Italy's Enel smart grid rollout).

1.10.1.4. **The Grid of the Future Will Be Autonomous, Intelligent, and Adaptive:**

- AI turns the grid into a predictive, self-healing ecosystem rather than a rigid infrastructure. In a time of pressing climate change and growing global energy consumption, this progression guarantees efficiency, resilience, and sustainability.

Chapter 2: Artificial Intelligence at the Core of Power Production

2.1. AI Enhancement for All Energy Sources

Artificial intelligence has evolved from a futuristic idea to a vital tool for increasing the efficiency of nuclear, fossil fuel, and renewable energy systems. AI algorithms can spot trends in massive volumes of operational data that human operators might overlook, allowing for real-time energy production optimization and waste reduction. *The production, management, and optimization of energy have all been completely transformed by artificial intelligence.* AI programs examine enormous datasets in all forms of power generation, including nuclear, renewables, and fossil fuels, to increase productivity, lower costs, and guarantee dependability.

2.2. Fossil Fuels Power Plants

AI anticipates the ideal fuel mix, modifies combustion processes, and optimizes turbine performance in conventional coal and natural gas plants. Machine learning algorithms, for instance, can help plants comply with ever-tougher environmental rules by balancing the trade-off between energy output and emissions.

Coal, natural gas, and oil-fired power plants are examples of *fossil fuel plants* that have long battled to balance emissions and efficiency. AI tackles this problem by:

- **Dynamic Fuel Optimization**: To find the ideal fuel mix that maximizes energy output while minimizing waste, machine learning algorithms examine fuel quality and combustion trends.
- **Emission Reduction**: AI continuously tracks particle and flue gas concentrations, modifying operations in real time to adhere to environmental regulations.
- **Load Balancing**: AI reduces fuel usage and operational strain by forecasting electricity demand and dynamically adjusting boiler and turbine outputs.

Example: A coal-fired plant that uses AI-driven optimization can minimize CO_2 emissions and fuel costs by 5–10% a year, which benefits the environment and the bottom line.

2.3. Nuclear Power Plants

Strict safety procedures and exact operational control are essential for nuclear power facilities. AI helps by keeping an eye on reactor conditions, anticipating any equipment malfunctions, and recommending ideal operating parameters. Predictive models can anticipate abnormalities in reactor coolant systems or turbine behaviour before they become serious problems by examining sensor and historical data.

Despite its remarkable efficiency, nuclear energy necessitates strict safety regulations and precise operational management. AI assists by:

- **Predictive Equipment Monitoring:** Reactor, coolant, and turbine irregularities are identified using machine learning models before they cause breakdowns.
- **Operating Efficiency**: To maximize reactor power levels without sacrificing safety, AI systems model various operating scenarios.
- **Maintenance Planning:** Strict safety regulations are upheld while avoidable downtime is avoided thanks to predictive analytics that guides maintenance plans.

Example: AI-assisted nuclear operations can predict minor mechanical problems days ahead of time, reducing the need for expensive shutdowns and increasing plant availability overall.

2.4. Sustainable Energy

Because they are highly dependent on the weather and surrounding conditions, wind, solar, and hydropower plants are inherently changeable. By using topographical mapping, historical production, and meteorological data, AI models predict energy generation, enabling utilities to plan energy dispatch and lessen need on backup fossil fuel plants.

Because of weather and environmental factors, renewable energy sources such as hydroelectric, solar, and wind power are inherently unpredictable. AI tackles these issues by:

- **Weather Forecasting**: By analysing meteorological data, machine learning algorithms are able to make highly accurate predictions about water flow, wind speed, and sunlight.
- **Grid Integration**: By maximizing when and how electricity is sent to the grid, AI assists utilities in managing the intermittent nature of renewable energy sources.
- **Performance Optimization**: To maximize energy capture, algorithms instantly modify the pitch of wind turbine blades or the position of solar panels.

Example: As an illustration of how predictive analytics can increase the dependability and economic viability of renewable energy, **Google DeepMind's** AI model increased the efficiency of wind farms in the **United Kingdom** by 20%.

2.5. Predictive Maintenance: The Application of Machine Learning

Predictive maintenance is among the most revolutionary uses of AI in power generating. Power plant maintenance has always been done according to set schedules or reactive interventions, both of which are frequently expensive and ineffective. This is altered by AI, which uses sensor data analysis to predict equipment failures before they happen.

- **How It Operates:** Data on temperature, vibration, pressure, and other operational characteristics are continuously gathered by sensors in boilers, generators, and turbines. By identifying minute departures from typical behaviour, machine learning models can anticipate possible malfunctions or wear and tear.
- **Advantages**: Predictive maintenance decreases operating expenses, increases equipment longevity, and minimizes unscheduled downtime.

Example: AI enables maintenance teams to step in at the right time to replace a turbine component after a catastrophic failure, saving millions of dollars in repairs and lost energy output.

2.6. Case Study: Wind Energy with Google DeepMind

Google DeepMind provides an impressive illustration of how AI is affecting renewable energy. The business collaborated with the National Grid of the United Kingdom to use machine learning to maximize wind power generation.

- **Difficulty:** Wind energy is unpredictable and extremely variable. The effectiveness of energy integration into the grid was constrained by conventional forecasting techniques.
- **AI Solution:** Predictive algorithms created by DeepMind examine past turbine data, current operating indicators, and weather forecasts. The system modifies turbine operations and informs grid dispatch methods by predicting wind patterns up to 36 hours in advance.
- **Outcomes:** This AI-powered method raised the amount of wind energy supplied to the grid by about 20%, illustrating how smart technologies may change renewable energy from a fluctuating source to a consistent power mix component.

By fusing operational effectiveness with predictive intelligence, artificial intelligence is revolutionizing power generation. *AI's ability to evaluate, forecast, and optimize energy sources—from fossil fuels to renewables—is not only increasing energy output but also laying the groundwork for a more intelligent, robust, and sustainable grid.*

Important Takeaway: AI serves as the plant's brain, enhancing its intelligence, cleanliness, and adaptability across all energy sources. AI turns conventional electricity generation into an effective and sustainable system by continuously evaluating data and forecasting results.

Chapter 3: Smarter Grid Distribution

The power grid's development has progressed beyond only delivering electricity. The distribution layer is currently being transformed by AI, which will make grids more intelligent, resilient, adaptive, and self-healing. Utilities can reduce blackouts, manage energy flow, and improve consumer reliability by utilizing real-time data, predictive algorithms, and intelligent control systems.

3.1. Using Real-Time Anomaly Detection to Find and Stop Blackouts

Conventional grids respond slowly to disruptions, which frequently leads to extensive outages. AI alters this by tracking grid performance continually and identifying irregularities before they become outages. Streams of sensor data are analysed by machine learning algorithms, which search for anomalous load patterns, frequency aberrations, or voltage changes.

- **Example: Pacific Gas & Electric (PG&E),** located in California, uses predictive analytics powered by artificial intelligence (AI) to find possible weak points in its distribution system. By anticipating equipment failures before they happen, this has helped shorten outage durations and shield millions of homes from unplanned blackouts.
- **Case Study: Smart Grid Pilot Projects in India:** By instantly warning operators of abnormal power decreases, AI-driven anomaly detection systems in Bangalore and Pune have decreased the frequency of localized blackouts by more than 30%.

3.2. AI-Powered Grids for Self-Healing and Fault Detection

AI is used by self-healing grids to automatically segregate and reroute power in addition to detecting faults. The AI system quickly locates the impacted area and takes corrective action, frequently without human assistance, when a problem arises, such as a fallen line or transformer failure.

- **Example:** Consider the **UK's National Grid**, where AI-driven energy management algorithms forecast regional electricity demand and modify power flows appropriately. AI can reroute electricity from regions with excess capacity during an unexpected spike in demand, lowering the possibility of blackouts.
- **South Korean Smart Cities**, such as Seoul, use artificial intelligence (AI) to balance conventional power plants with dispersed renewable energy sources like solar and wind. By prioritizing renewable energy when it is available, intelligent routing algorithms improve sustainability and save operating expenses.

Diagram: Cybersecurity in AI-Powered Grids

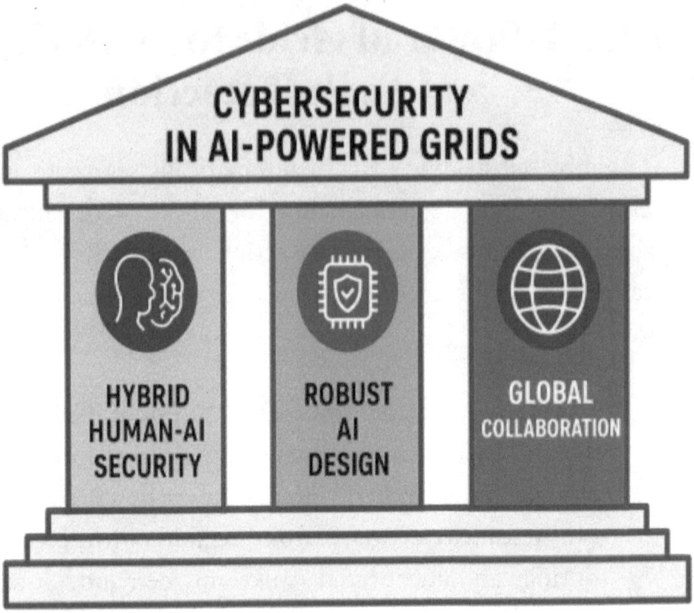

Figure 2: Cybersecurity in AI-Powered Grids

3.3. The Path Forward: Self-governing, Flexible Distribution

Fully autonomous distribution networks are made possible by the integration of intelligent routing, anomaly monitoring, and AI-powered defect detection. Grids of the future will be able to:

- Self-optimization in response to generation and load circumstances.
- Streamlining the integration of dispersed energy sources.
- Giving renewables priority to reduce carbon footprints.
- Constantly learning from operational data to improve productivity.

3.4. Self-Optimization according to Generation and Load Conditions

Grids nowadays are dynamic networks. Self-optimization is made possible by AI, which enables the grid to continuously modify operations in response to supply (generation) and demand (load) conditions.

Specifics and the Mechanism:

- Real-time data from generating facilities, substations, and smart meters is tracked by AI algorithms.
- The system makes dynamic distribution adjustments by examining patterns of consumption, energy storage levels, and generation capacity.
- AI can, for instance, activate energy storage devices or redirect power from unused lines during periods of high demand.

Case Studies:

- **UK Grid & Google DeepMind:** AI algorithms were able to manage electricity usage almost instantly, lowering the grid's stress from peak loads and enhancing dependability.
- **E.ON's Digital Grid in Germany:** The utility use AI to minimize transmission losses, dynamically regulate voltage, and balance load in metropolitan areas.

  Impact:

  - Lowers the possibility of blackouts during periods of high demand; • Increases efficiency by cutting down on energy waste.
  - Reduces utility operating expenses.

3.5. Distributed Energy Resources (DERs) Integration Easily

A more decentralized energy environment is produced by the growth of Microgrids, wind farms, and rooftop solar. AI makes sure that these dispersed resources seamlessly connect to the main grid.

Details and Mechanism:

- AI uses historical patterns, consumption trends, and weather projections to forecast energy generation from solar panels, wind turbines, and battery storage.
- To maximize total energy flow, the system determines when to store, use, or return energy back into the grid.
- To ensure frequency and voltage stability, DERs can be sent out automatically.

Examples of Cases:

- **California ISO:** Artificial intelligence forecasts rooftop solar output and automatically strikes a balance between distributed solar energy and grid demand to avoid interruptions.
- **Hornsdale Power Reserve in Australia**: AI oversees one of the biggest battery storage systems globally, combining it with solar and wind power to offer responsive grid support.

Impact:

- Facilitates the dependable incorporation of renewable energy.
- Increases grid resilience in the event of unplanned generation outages.
- Promotes the use of Microgrids in both rural and urban

settings

Diagram: Grid Distribution Gets Smarter

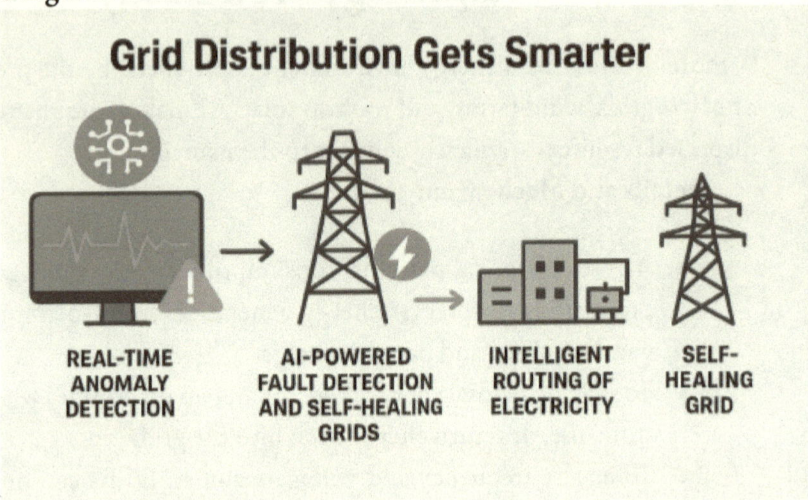

Figure 3: Grid Distribution Gets Smarter

3.6. Making Renewables a Priority to Reduce Carbon Footprints

AI makes it possible for the grid to reliably select low-carbon energy sources. It guarantees that renewables are used as efficiently as possible by examining patterns of generation, storage, and demand.

Specifics and the Mechanism:

- AI predicts when solar or wind power will be at its highest and modifies energy dispatch to optimize the usage of renewable resources.
- Why? By only running when required, fossil fuel plants lower carbon emissions.
- By forecasting the availability of renewable resources, machine learning models can reduce dependency on polluting sources.

Examples of Cases:

- **Google's Data Centres:** AI optimizes the use of renewable energy by coordinating data centre demands with times when renewable power is at its highest. Carbon intensity significantly decreased as a result.
- **Iberdrola (Spain):** Reduces CO_2 emissions by millions of tons yearly by optimizing wind and solar output across its portfolio using AI.

Impact:

- Encourages decarbonisation initiatives and climate aims.
- Increases the predictability and dependability of renewable energy.

- Lowers operating expenses by reducing reliance on fossil fuels.

3.7. Constantly Gaining Knowledge from Operational Data to Increase Productivity

AI systems learn over time and becoming smarter as they process more operational data; they don't merely react.

Specifics and the Mechanism:

- AI examines grid data in real time and in the past to find trends, irregularities, and inefficiencies.
- By experimenting with routing, load balancing, and storage deployment, reinforcement learning enables AI to progressively enhance performance.
- Predictive maintenance algorithms minimize downtime by anticipating faults before they happen.

Examples include:

- **Siemens Spectrum Power**, which optimizes transformer load and maintenance schedules to prolong equipment life and lower failure rates by using AI to continuously learn from grid performance.
- **Enel Smart Grid Project (Italy):** AI predicts and prevents breakdowns by analysing years of operating data, increasing efficiency and lowering energy losses.

Impact:

- Constant enhancement of grid functionality.
- Fewer outages and lower operating expenses.
- Over time, more intelligent integration of new energy technologies.

Key Takeaway: AI lays the groundwork for future energy networks by enabling the grid to become autonomous, robust, and ecologically sustainable through the combination of self-optimization, DER integration, renewable prioritizing, and continuous learning.

The four AI-driven smart grid capabilities are summarized in the following table, which also includes examples, procedures, and effects:

Diagram: The Four AI-Driven Smart Grid Capabilities

Capability	Mechanism	Case Studies	Impact / Benefits
Self-Optimizing Based on Load and Generation Conditions	AI monitors real-time data from smart meters, substations, and generation plants; dynamically adjusts distribution to match supply and demand	- Google DeepMind & UK Grid: Optimized electricity usage in near real-time - E.ON Digital Grid, Germany: Balanced urban load, minimized transmission losses	- Reduces blackout risks - Improves efficiency and reduces energy waste - Lowers operational costs
Integrating Distributed Energy Resources (DERs) Seamlessly	AI predicts energy generation from solar, wind, and storage; decides when to store, use, or feed energy into the grid; stabilizes voltage and frequency	- California ISO: Balances rooftop solar output with grid demand - Hornsdale Power Reserve, Australia: Manages battery storage with wind and solar integration	- Enhances renewable adoption - Improves grid reliability and resilience - Enables Microgrid deployment

Capability	Mechanism	Case Studies	Impact / Benefits
Minimizing Carbon Footprints by Prioritizing Renewables	AI forecasts high renewable generation periods; adjusts energy dispatch to maximize renewables and minimize fossil fuel use	- Google Data Centres: Aligns loads with renewable availability to reduce carbon intensity - Iberdrola, Spain: Optimizes wind and solar output to cut CO_2 emissions	- Supports decarbonisation goals - Reduces reliance on fossil fuels - Lowers operational costs
Learning Continuously from Operational Data to Enhance Efficiency	AI analyses historical and real-time data to detect patterns, optimize load routing, and predict failures; reinforcement learning improves decisions over time	- Siemens Spectrum Power: Optimizes transformer load and maintenance schedules - Enel Smart Grid, Italy: Predicts and prevents failures, reducing energy losses	- Continuous grid performance improvement - Fewer outages and lower maintenance costs - Smarter integration of new energy technologies

Figure 4: The four AI-driven smart grid capabilities

In summary, artificial intelligence is changing grid distribution from a reactive system to an intelligent, proactive network. In addition to preventing blackouts, smart grids are laying the groundwork for a robust, sustainable energy future by identifying abnormalities, isolating faults, and dynamically routing electricity.

Chapter 4: Forecasting Demand and Optimizing Consumption

Overview

Energy systems of today are about knowing *how, where, and when energy is used*, and not just about sending electricity. At the heart of this transformation are demand forecasting and consumption optimization, which enable utilities to effectively balance supply and demand while lowering expenses and carbon footprints. *In order for electricity suppliers to anticipate energy consumption and effectively manage supply, demand forecasting and consumption optimization are essential elements of the smart grid revolution.* Utility companies are able to obtain comprehensive insights into the consumption habits of households, businesses, and entire cities by utilizing *real-time data from smart meters and IoT-enabled devices.*

This data is processed by *machine learning algorithms*, which take into consideration factors like occupancy, weather, and seasonal patterns to produce precise projections. Demand-side management is strengthened by these projections, which enable networks to optimize energy distribution, balance loads, and lower peak demand. Examples from around the world show how effective these methods are:

- **Tokyo**: Incorporates smart meters and AI to modify industrial energy use during peak periods, decreasing demand spikes and enhancing grid resilience;
- **Singapore**: Employs AI to forecast city-wide demand in 15-minute intervals, allowing dynamic load shifting and lowering peak use.

Predictive analytics, automatic usage optimization, and real-time monitoring work together to:

- Reduce carbon emissions,
- Improve grid stability,

- Save operating costs, and
- Increase consumer involvement through intelligent energy management.

The grid is essentially changed from a reactive system to a proactive, adaptable network that can satisfy the demands of contemporary, energy-hungry cities through demand forecasting and consumption optimization.

4.1. Grid Stability

The foundation of every dependable electrical system is grid stability. By anticipating consumption peaks and troughs, demand forecasting helps utilities avoid overloads and blackouts. Operators can proactively redistribute power, turn on backup systems, or install energy storage devices by anticipating when and where electricity will be needed.

- **Example:** AI-driven demand management in Tokyo smoothes out spikes that can cause grid instability by moving industrial energy use away from peak hours.

- In **Singapore**, real-time monitoring enables operators to automatically lower or postpone non-essential loads during times of high demand, ensuring a consistent and dependable supply.
- **Impact:** Fewer blackouts, less stress on infrastructure, and better ability to handle unforeseen events like heat waves or natural disasters.

4.2. Lower Costs of Doing Business

Precise demand forecasting saves energy waste and eliminates the need for costly standby generation. Power plant scheduling can be optimized by utilities, which can also prevent overproduction and schedule repairs at times of low demand rather than high demand.

Examples include:

- Predictive algorithms are used by European smart grids to determine which plants should operate and when, saving millions of dollars in fuel and operating expenses.
- Dynamic load balancing lessens the need for peaking power plants, which are usually more costly and inefficient to run.

Impact: More economical energy generation, less infrastructure deterioration, and more effective resource distribution.

4.3. Reduced Emissions of Carbon

Demand-side management minimizes the need for carbon-intensive peaking plants and promotes the use of renewable energy sources by managing electricity use.

In order to reduce dependency on fossil fuels, machine learning models can predict when renewable generation (wind, solar) will be enough and adjust loads accordingly.

Examples include:

- California uses less natural gas because AI forecasts solar production output and automatically schedules high-energy activities for the day.
- By lowering peak loads, Tokyo's smart grid lessens the need for emergency fossil fuel generators.

Impact: Better air quality, lower greenhouse gas emissions, and advancement toward national and decarbonisation goals.

4.4. Smart Energy Management for Better Customer Engagement

In order to maximize energy use, consumers are crucial. Real-time feedback on electricity consumption is provided by smart meters and Internet of Things-enabled devices, allowing businesses and consumers to modify their practices for efficiency and cost savings. By providing incentives for dynamic pricing, utilities can persuade customers to divert their use from peak hours.

Examples:

- In **Singapore**, citizens take part in city-wide demand management by receiving notifications and recommendations to use less energy during periods of high demand.
- In the **United States**, smart thermostats automatically modify heating and cooling schedules in response to anticipated electricity rates, which lowers demand and bills overall.

Impact: By actively participating in energy management, consumers help the grid run more sustainably and effectively while also saving money.

4.5. IoT-Enabled Homes and Smart Meters as Sources of Real-Time Data

Accurate and detailed data collection is the first step towards successful demand forecasting. Monthly usage data from traditional energy meters is insufficient for dynamic grid management. IoT-enabled houses and smart meters enable utilities to track electricity consumption in real time:

- **Smart Meters:** These gadgets communicate data to utilities every few minutes, tracking electricity usage at the level of specific homes or commercial buildings. They record periods of high demand, allowing for accurate load control.
- **IoT-Powered Houses:** Continuous feedback on usage trends is provided by sensors and connected appliances, such as EV chargers, water heaters, and smart thermostats. This data can be compiled by utilities to spot patterns in behaviour and forecast demand in the future.

4.5.1. Smart Meters

Smart meters are cutting-edge energy metering systems that send data to utilities instantly after recording electricity usage in real time. Smart meters are essential to contemporary, data-driven energy management because they offer detailed, time-stamped insights into energy consumption, in contrast to traditional meters that only provide monthly readings.

4.5.1.1. Important Features

- **Real-Time Monitoring:** Keep tabs on energy usage at 5- to 15-minute intervals.
- **Two-Way Communication**: Enables utilities to transmit data, such demand-response directives or dynamic pricing signals, back to the meter.
- **Remote Configuration:** Without sending technicians to the location, utilities can change settings or update firmware remotely.
- **IoT Device Integration:** To maximize energy use in a home or building, smart appliances, thermostats, and EV chargers can be connected.

4.5.1.2. Benefits

a. **Better Demand Forecasting**: Accurate consumption information aids in the prediction of peak loads and the effective planning of generation.
b. **Improved Grid Stability:** Utilities are able to react fast to abrupt increases or decreases in demand.
c. **Consumer Empowerment:** Businesses and households can compare prices, keep an eye on energy consumption, and

modify their behaviour to save money.

d. **Support for Renewable Integration:** Makes it possible to better match times of high renewable generation with energy use.

4.6. Case Studies

- **Japan:** AI algorithms that optimize urban grid loads and avoid blackouts are fed data from smart meters that record electricity use every 15 minutes.
- **United Kingdom:** Smart meters are used in millions of homes to enable dynamic pricing schemes that promote energy use during off-peak hours and lower peak demand.
- **United States (California):** Smart meters assist customers lower their energy costs and carbon footprints by integrating with utility apps to offer real-time consumption feedback and incentives.

4.7. IoT-Enabled Homes

Real-time energy consumption monitoring and control are made possible by an interconnected network of *Sensors and Devices*. These smart houses provide detailed insights that help utilities and consumers optimize energy use effectively, making them an essential data layer in contemporary energy systems.

4.7.1. Important Features

- **Linked Appliances:** Intelligent water heaters, washing machines, HVAC systems, and refrigerators can be set to run at off-peak times or when renewable energy sources are plentiful.
- **Smart Lighting and Thermostats**: These devices automatically change the lighting, heating, and cooling according to occupancy, the time of day, and the weather.
- **Energy Monitoring Dashboards**: Using apps, homeowners can monitor their energy usage, get warnings, and get suggestions for energy and money-saving measures.
- **Integration with Smart Meters:** AI algorithms use usage data from IoT devices to estimate demand and dynamically balance loads in the central grid.

4.7.2. Advantages

a. **Increased Energy Efficiency:** Unnecessary energy use is decreased via automated appliance control.

b. **Consumer Engagement**: Motivated by immediate feedback and recommendations, residents actively take part in energy-saving projects.

c. **Demand Response Support**: In reaction to utility signals, homes can automatically lower or change their energy consumption during peak hours.
d. **Alignment with Renewable Generation**: To maximize the integration of renewable energy sources, devices can be programmed to use power when solar or wind output is high.

4.7.3. Case Studies

- **Singapore:** To maximize energy utilization, *IoT-enabled households connect to the city's smart grid*. Peak electricity use can be reduced by 5–10% thanks to AI algorithms that modify HVAC and appliance operation to lower peak load.
- **Tokyo:** Dynamic pricing schemes complement residential IoT devices. To ease the burden on the grid, households move energy-intensive tasks like water heating and laundry to off-peak hours.
- **United States:** By scheduling appliance operations according to electricity prices, smart home platforms such as Nest and Ecobee help homeowners cut expenses and peak demand.

4.8. Using Machine Learning to Forecast Consumption Trends

Following data collection, electricity consumption is predicted at several sizes, including home, industrial, and citywide, using machine learning (ML) algorithms. Economic activity, occupancy patterns, weather, and seasonal variations can all be taken into account by ML models.

Important methods consist of:

- **Time-Series Analysis**: Both short- and long-term consumption trends are predicted using algorithms such as LSTM (Long Short-Term Memory) networks.
- **Clustering and Segmentation**: Based on usage trends, households and businesses are classified to enable customized demand-response tactics.
- **Predictive Load Balancing**: ML models identify the best way to distribute electricity throughout the grid by using historical data, energy pricing, and weather forecasts.

4.8.1. Time-Series Analysis

A statistical and machine learning technique called time-series analysis looks at past consumption data over time to predict electricity demand. Time-series models are perfect for forecasting both short- and long-term trends since energy usage patterns frequently follow daily, weekly, and seasonal cycles.

Important Methods:

- **Auto-Regressive Integrated Moving Average (ARIMA):**

Measures seasonality and linear patterns in electricity use.

- **LSTM (Long Short-Term Memory) Networks:** Recurrent neural networks of the LSTM network type are particularly good at spotting long-term relationships in sequential data, including multi-day or seasonal energy patterns.
- **Prophet:** A time-series forecasting algorithm created by Facebook that effectively manages daily, weekly, and holiday effects.

Applications:

Include scheduling smart appliances by forecasting household electricity consumption at 15-minute intervals.

- Predicting industrial demand to avoid overloads during times of high output.
- Predicting the city's overall electrical load to schedule generation and storage requirements.

Case Study: Time-series models in Singapore forecast energy usage across the city, enabling AI systems to automatically move non-essential loads during peak hours and enhancing grid stability.

4.9. Segmentation and Clustering

Devices or customers are grouped by clustering and segmentation according to comparable patterns of energy use. Utilities can enhance forecasting precision, create customized services for various client categories, and create tailored demand-response tactics by examining these clusters.

Important Methods:

- **K-Means Clustering:** Assembles companies or families with comparable daily or weekly energy profiles.
- **Hierarchical Clustering:** This method distinguishes between the commercial, industrial, and residential sectors by identifying nested patterns in energy consumption.
- **Density-Based Spatial Clustering (DBSCAN):** Finds atypical clusters, including residences with wildly fluctuating energy usage.

Applications include:

- Dividing households into "high-usage" and "low-usage" groups to provide tailored energy-saving advice.
- To improve scheduling, find industrial facilities with comparable load patterns.
- Identifying irregularities that could point to equipment problems, like abrupt increases in energy consumption.

Case Study: Tokyo classifies residential and business customers using clustering, which allows for tailored incentives for load shifting and effective demand-side management.

4.10. Predictive Load Balancing

By using AI and ML to dynamically distribute electricity throughout the grid in response to anticipated demand, predictive load balancing makes sure that supply keeps up with demand while reducing the strain on infrastructure. It proactively redistributes energy or initiates demand-response operations in anticipation of peak demands.

Important Methods:

- **Optimization Algorithms:** Heuristic and linear programming techniques distribute energy to reduce expenses and prevent overloading transformers or lines.
- **Reinforcement Learning**: With time and grid feedback, AI agents learn the best load distribution techniques.
- **Hybrid Models:** For adaptive load balancing, combine real-time grid data, clustering insights, and time-series forecasts.

Applications include:

- Preventing blackouts by automatically lowering or postponing non-essential loads during peak hours.
- For optimal efficiency, coordinating dispersed energy resources like battery storage and rooftop solar.
- Encouraging the integration of renewable energy sources by coordinating consumption with times when solar or wind power is most abundant.

Case Study: By allowing utilities to move energy-intensive operations in industrial zones to off-peak times, predictive load balancing helps California reduce peak demand and its need on fossil fuel peaking units.

4.11. Automatic Regression Integrated Moving Average (ARIMA)

A popular statistical technique for predicting time-series data, like power use, is ARIMA. It *uses differencing to make the data stationary (integrated portion), historical forecast mistakes (moving average part), and historical values (autoregressive part) to model a variable.*

Important Characteristics include:

- **Captures Linear Trends**: This feature is great for seeing steady, linear trends in energy consumption over time.
- **Seasonality Handling**: To account for seasonal fluctuations, such as daily or annual cycles in electricity usage, ARIMA can be expanded (as SARIMA).
- **Short-Term Forecasting:** Effective for prediction horizons that are short to medium.

Applications include:

- Scheduling smart appliances based on daily domestic electricity demand predictions.
- Projecting industrial energy usage for operational planning purposes.

Example: European utilities employ ARIMA models to predict the amount of electricity that will be needed over the course of the following 24 to 48 hours. This allows power plants to be dispatched efficiently and lessens the need for costly peaking generation.

4.12. Long Short-Term Memory (LSTM) Networks

A particular kind of *Recurrent Neural Network* (RNN) called an LSTM network is made especially to process sequential input with long-term dependencies. LSTMs are *perfect for complex energy usage patterns that span several days or seasons because they can retain information over extended periods of time,* unlike typical RNNs.

Important Attributes:

- **Memory Cells and Gates**: LSTMs can simulate intricate temporal connections by using input, output, and forget gates to determine what data to keep or discard.
- **Managing Nonlinear Trends**: captures irregular and nonlinear trends in energy use that may be missed by traditional models such as ARIMA.
- **Scalable:** Able to manage massive datasets from citywide grids, industrial areas, and IoT-enabled houses.

Applications include:

- Demand-response scheduling optimization using multi-day household consumption forecasting.
- Forecasting energy consumption in smart cities by using event, occupancy, and weather patterns.

Example: LSTM models in Singapore predict the city's energy consumption every 15 minutes, allowing for AI-powered load shifting and increased grid stability.

4.13. Prophet

Facebook created **Prophet,** an open-source forecasting tool, to make time-series predictions simple, understandable, and reliable, especially for operational or commercial data. It uses a combination of trend, seasonality, and holidays or other special events to model time-series data.

Important Attributes:

- **Manages Daily, Weekly, and Annual Seasonality**: Adapts to various seasonal trends in power consumption automatically.
- **Robust to Outliers and Missing Data:** Even with erratic or insufficient data, it is still possible to produce accurate forecasts.
- **User-Friendly:** Unlike ARIMA or LSTM, it requires less statistical knowledge, making it accessible to energy managers or utilities.

Applications include:

- Predicting electricity usage in homes or businesses while accounting for holidays and seasonal variations.
- Combining weather-related events with special occasions (like festivals or sporting events) that impact energy use.

Example: U.S. utilities have employed Prophet to forecast electricity demand during holidays and severe weather, enabling proactive energy allocation and peak load control.

Diagram: Table Clearly Comparing ARIMA, LSTM, and Prophet:

In the context of forecasting power consumption, the following table clearly compares ARIMA, LSTM, and Prophet:

Method	Description	Strengths	Weaknesses	Best Use Cases
ARIMA (Auto-Regressive Integrated Moving Average)	Classical statistical model that uses past values, forecast errors, and differencing to predict future trends.	- Captures linear trends - Good for short- to medium-term forecasts - Handles seasonal data with SARIMA extension	- Struggles with nonlinear or highly irregular patterns - Sensitive to missing data - Requires stationary data	- Short-term residential load forecasting - Industrial energy planning with predictable patterns
LSTM (Long Short-Term Memory) Networks	Recurrent neural network that remembers long-term dependencies in sequential data.	- Captures nonlinear and complex patterns - Handles long-term dependencies - Scalable for large datasets	- Computationally intensive - Requires large amounts of training data - Harder to interpret	- City-wide or multi-day forecasting - IoT-enabled home or industrial zone demand prediction
Prophet	Open-source forecasting tool by Facebook combining trend, seasonality, and holidays/	- Handles daily, weekly, yearly seasonality - Robust to missing data and outliers - Easy to use	- Less effective for highly irregular or high-frequency data - May underperform on very short-term forecasts	- Household and commercial consumption with seasonal patterns - Predicting

Method	Description	Strengths	Weaknesses	Best Use Cases
	special events.	and interpret		demand around holidays or special events

Figure 5: Table Clearly Comparing ARIMA, LSTM, and Prophet

4.14. Case Studies of AI Demand-Side Management

a. **Singapore: Smart Urban Grids**

- Millions of IoT devices' real-time data is integrated into Singapore's Smart Nation plan.
- AI anticipates hours of high demand and automatically modifies non-essential loads, such water heating or air cooling, during those times.
- **Result**: A 5–10% decrease in peak electricity demand, enhanced grid stability, and decreased operating expenses.

a. **Tokyo: Optimizing Urban Energy**

- Predictive energy allocation in industrial zones is made possible by Tokyo's Cap-and-Trade program in conjunction with smart meters.
- AI examines patterns in energy use and automatically notifies offices and factories to move energy-intensive operations to off-peak hours.
- **Result:** By reducing electricity spikes by 15%, peak shaving helped to avoid expensive infrastructure changes.

4.15. Advantages of Consumption Optimization and Demand Forecasting

Variable demand, the incorporation of renewable energy sources, and the requirement for sustainable operations have made modern energy systems more complex. These issues are addressed by *demand forecasting and consumption optimization*, which offer utilities and customers useful information with several advantages:

4.15.1. Grid Stability

Utilities can proactively regulate supply and avoid overloads or blackouts by using demand forecasting to predict electricity usage. Grid managers can guarantee smooth power flow throughout the network by anticipating peak loads and modifying generation, storage, and distribution beforehand.

Important effects include:

- Lowers the possibility of blackouts during severe weather or unforeseen increases in consumption.
- By modifying demand patterns to correspond with availability, it facilitates the incorporation of intermittent renewable energy sources and keeps transformers, transmission lines, and substations from overloading.

Example: Load-shifting techniques that preserve grid stability even during heatwaves are made possible in Tokyo by AI-driven demand management that forecasts industrial and residential energy peaks.

4.15.2. Cost Efficiency

Demand forecasting enables utilities to minimize wasteful operating expenses and maximize electricity generation. Operators can more effectively manage generation, schedule maintenance during periods of low demand, and avoid expensive infrastructure upgrades by not excessively depending on pricey peaking facilities.

Important effects include:

- Lowers fuel usage and power plant wear.
- Reduces the need to invest in extra capacity that might only be utilized occasionally.
- Optimizes the deployment of dispersed energy sources, including rooftop solar or battery storage.

Example: European utilities schedule combined heat and power plants using predictive analytics, which reduces their need on expensive peaking generators and saves millions of dollars yearly.

4.15.3. Environmental Impact

Carbon emissions can also be decreased by anticipating demand and optimizing use. The energy system becomes more sustainable by increasing the use of renewable generation and decreasing reliance on fossil-fuel peaking plants.

Important effects include:

- Lowers local air pollution and greenhouse gas emissions;
- Lowers the carbon footprint of emergency generating during periods of high demand; and
- Promotes the integration of distributed energy resources such

as energy storage, wind, and solar.

Example: California's AI-driven demand-response programs reduce the need for natural gas generation and CO2 emissions by scheduling high-energy activities during the peak of solar production.

4.15.4. Empowerment of Consumers

Customers have direct control over how much energy they use because to dynamic pricing, smart meters, and IoT-enabled gadgets. Businesses and consumers can participate in grid management, modify behaviour, and save money via real-time feedback.

Key effects include:

- Businesses can manage production schedules to minimize energy costs;
- Households respond to price signals by shifting energy-intensive activities to off-peak hours; and
- Promotes the adoption of energy-efficient appliances and habits.

Example: In **Singapore,** citizens are notified when electricity usage peaks and are encouraged to cut back, which lowers demand throughout the city and lowers electricity costs.

Chapter 5: Forecasting Renewable Energy: Predicting the Unpredictable

Overview

5.1. The Problem: Wind and Solar Unpredictability

The inherent variability of renewable energy sources, such as wind and solar power, makes grid management considerably more difficult than it is for conventional fossil fuel generation. In contrast to coal or gas facilities, which can produce a steady, predictable output, wind turbines and solar panels are dependent on environmental elements like weather.

5.1.1. Intermittent Behaviour and Its Effects

- **Solar Power**: *Sunlight, which is dependent on cloud cover, seasonal fluctuations, and day-night cycles, is what drives solar generation*. Within minutes, production can be drastically reduced by even momentary clouds.
- **Wind Power:** The *direction and speed of the wind have a significant impact on wind energy*. Turbines risk mechanical strain during gusts or turbulence and produce less power during calm conditions.
- **Grid Repercussions:** These variations make it difficult to balance supply and demand, raising the possibility of blackouts, voltage instability, and power shortages.

Example: The "*duck curve*" in California shows how solar power drops sharply in the evening, necessitating a quick ramp-up from fossil fuel plants to keep up with demand.

5.2. Operational Challenges

5.2.1. **Grid instability:** Power quality may be impacted by abrupt drops or increases in renewable energy production, which can cause frequency and voltage instability.

5.2.2. **Need for Backup Generation:** Utilities frequently use hydro or fossil fuel backup to make up for unpredictability, which raises expenses and emissions.

5.2.3. **Energy Curtailment:** In order to avoid overloading the grid and wasting clean energy during periods of excessive generation, renewable energy must be reduced.

5.3. The Importance of Accurate Forecasting

Predicting variability before it occurs is the answer.

Operators can:

- Modify energy storage and dispatch beforehand with accurate predictions.
- Control variable loads to maintain supply and demand equilibrium.
- Minimize the reduction of surplus renewable energy and lessen dependency on fossil fuel backup.

AI-powered forecasting solves the intrinsic unpredictability of solar and wind, converting these erratic resources into dependable, grid-friendly energy sources that promote greater adoption of renewable energy sources and lower carbon emissions worldwide.

By their very nature, renewable energy sources such as wind and solar are sporadic. Wind turbines rely on wind direction and speed, while solar panels rely on sunlight, unlike fossil fuel facilities that may increase output on demand.

The stability of the grid is seriously threatened by these fluctuations:

- In just a few minutes, **sudden cloud cover** can drastically lower solar output.
- Wind farms may operate poorly due to **shifting wind patterns**, which could impact the reliability of the power supply.

- Unanticipated, **overproduction** at periods of high renewable power could overburden the grid.

Germany's **Energiewende** program, for instance, has brought attention to the challenges of supply balancing when solar energy peaks in the middle of the day and declines in the evening, necessitating quick adjustments from traditional power plants.

5.4. Artificial Intelligence for Renewable Prediction

By accurately forecasting the generation of renewable energy, artificial intelligence and machine learning provide answers. Important uses consist of:

a. **Weather Modelling:**

- *Artificial Intelligence* (AI) models use enormous datasets, such as satellite imagery, historical weather data, and atmospheric patterns, to predict wind speed and sun irradiance hours or even days ahead of time.
- *Neutral Networks* are able to identify subtle patterns that traditional models frequently overlook, like coastal wind shear or the effects of urban microclimates.

a. **Cloud Prediction:**

- Grid operators can anticipate solar drops and make proactive adjustments to storage systems or auxiliary generation by using sophisticated computer vision algorithms that scan satellite and ground-based camera data to predict cloud movement and density.

a. **3. Analysis of Wind Patterns:**

- In order to maximize turbine blade angles and energy collection, machine learning algorithms forecast sustained wind patterns, gusts, and turbulence.
- Additionally, predictive maintenance scheduling may be synchronized with wind forecasts, which lowers downtime

and increases dependability.

5.5. A Case Study: IBM's Hybrid Renewable Energy Forecasting (HREF) System:

An innovative illustration of how artificial intelligence (AI) might revolutionize the integration of renewable energy sources is **IBM's Hybrid Renewable Energy Forecasting (HREF)** technology. HREF increases prediction accuracy by fusing real-time sensor data, complex weather modelling, and cutting-edge machine learning algorithms, allowing utilities to run cleaner and smarter grids.

5.5.1. **Combining Various Data Sources**:

HREF's capacity to absorb and combine many datasets to produce a thorough picture of the state of energy generation both now and in the future is one of its main advantages:

- **Satellite Imagery**: Offers high-level information on regional weather patterns, solar irradiance, and cloud cover.
- **Weather Station Data:** Provides high-resolution, localized measurements of temperature, humidity, wind speed, and other environmental parameters that affect the production of renewable energy.
- **Wind Turbine and Solar Panel Logs:** Forecasts and production irregularities can be detected with the use of real-time operational data from wind turbines and solar arrays.

Combining these datasets allows HREF to produce forecasts that are more accurate than those produced by conventional models by taking into consideration both local microclimate impacts and broad-scale meteorological patterns.

5.5.2. **Machine Learning Models:**

HREF predicts renewable energy generation by utilizing ensemble learning techniques and neural networks:

- **Short- and Medium-Term Forecasts:** Grid operators can proactively prepare for swings by using the system's 48-hour forecast of solar and wind generation.
- **Pattern Recognition:** By learning from past data, AI algorithms are able to spot minute relationships between geography, weather patterns, and the production of renewable energy.
- **Continuous Improvement**: By comparing predicted output to generation, machine learning algorithms continuously improve predictions, increasing accuracy over time.

For high-renewable grids to remain stable, this skill allows for predictive grid management as opposed to reactive modifications.

5.5.3. Effect on Grid Functions

For utilities, the implementation of HREF offers immediate operational and financial advantages:

- **Less Reliance on Fossil Backup:** Utilities can reduce their reliance on gas or coal facilities, reducing emissions and fuel expenses, by precisely forecasting renewable output.
- **Reduced Energy Curtailment**: By enabling utilities to capture more renewable energy, HREF helps to ensure energy is used efficiently and minimize waste from overproduction.
- **Enhanced Grid Efficiency:** Precise forecasting aids in supply

and demand balancing, overload prevention, and storage dispatch optimization.

- **Example:** Compared to conventional statistical models, HREF significantly improved forecasting errors for renewable energy by 30% in a test run with a large U.S. utility.

This made it possible for wind and solar energy to be integrated into the grid more smoothly; it also reduced operating costs, reduced the need for fossil fuel backups, and increased system stability overall.

5.5.4. **Important Takeaways**

IBM's HREF serves as an example of how hybrid forecasting driven by AI might transform the integration of renewable energy:

a. **Data Fusion:** Highly accurate forecasts are produced by combining operational, weather, and satellite data.
b. **Predictive Intelligence:** Real-time optimization and proactive grid management are made possible by machine learning.
c. **Sustainability Impact**: HREF promotes a cleaner, more robust energy system by lowering reliance on fossil fuels and minimizing energy curtailment.

This case study demonstrates a larger trend: AI is actively facilitating smarter, greener, and more efficient grids globally, not only forecasting renewable energy.

5.6. Predictive Renewable Management's Future

The future of renewable energy is about intelligent, dynamic, and global energy management, not just about building more solar panels or wind turbines. Energy systems are becoming more sustainable, resilient, and efficient as a result of developments in artificial intelligence and predictive analytics:

5.6.1. **Adjustments in Real Time: Improved, Quicker, Self-Sustained Energy Movement**

Energy systems can react immediately to changes in renewable supply and demand thanks to AI's ability to enable real-time adjustments throughout the grid:

- **Automated Energy Storage and Dispatch:** AI predicts spikes in wind or solar power and routes extra energy to pumped hydro, batteries, or other storage devices. To keep the system stable during anticipated drops, stored energy is released right away:

- **Dynamic Load Balancing**: Smart grids can send signals to adapt energy use in real time, such as to water pumping stations, electric vehicle chargers, or industrial facilities. This maintains supply and demand equilibrium without the need for human involvement.
- **Predictive Maintenance Integration**: By using predicted generation to estimate equipment strain, AI can proactively schedule maintenance to prevent downtime.

Impact: Blackouts and energy waste are decreased as grids become self-correcting systems that can continue to function even in the face of abrupt weather changes.

Example: AI-controlled battery dispatch and load shifting are helping to alleviate California's "duck curve" issue, where solar output drops off significantly in the evening, averting energy shortages and lowering the state's reliance on fossil fuel backup.

5.6.2. Forecasting Hybrid Energy: Managing Several Renewable Resources

AI enables operators to optimize the overall grid ecology by managing multiple energy sources at once:

- **Cross-Source Optimization:** AI systems combine data from solar, wind, hydro, and batteries to determine which energy source should be used at any given moment. For instance, hydro or stored solar energy can instantly make up for a decline in wind production.
- **Energy Storage Management**: AI anticipates storage requirements ahead of time, minimizing needless reductions in renewable energy production and optimizing efficiency.
- **Grid-wide Coordination**: AI has the ability to synchronize energy across nations or regions, allowing excess energy in one place to compensate for shortages in another.

Impact: Grids become a fully integrated, intelligent energy ecosystem that can manage increased renewable penetration while retaining dependability, rather than a collection of disparate, autonomous sources.

Example: By integrating offshore wind, solar farms, and pumped hydro storage, the European energy grid uses hybrid AI forecasting, enabling nations like Germany and Denmark to maximize renewable use while maintaining a steady energy supply.

5.6.3. Consequences: Motivating Decarbonisation Worldwide

Global AI-driven renewable forecasting significantly affects energy policy and the climate, with far-reaching effects that go beyond local efficiency:

- **Less Fossil Backup:** Precise forecasts eliminate the need for coal or gas facilities to be kept on standby, which lowers operating expenses and greenhouse gas emissions.
- **Greater Renewable Penetration**: AI speeds up the world's transition to clean energy by enabling grids to include more sporadic renewables without sacrificing stability.
- **Climate Resilience:** AI guarantees a steady supply of electricity in locations with erratic weather patterns, enabling the adoption of renewable energy in emerging countries and energy-poor regions.
- **International Case Study:** AI-based forecasting for wind and solar farms in India lowers energy curtailment, lowers the need for diesel backup, and advances the country's decarbonisation objectives.

Impact: AI becomes a key component of a sustainable, resilient, and decarbonized global energy system by lowering reliance on fossil fuels, coordinating a variety of energy sources, and facilitating quick real-time adjustments.

5.6.4. The Path Ahead

Predictive renewable management will keep developing in the future:

- **Integration with Smart Cities:** To maximize urban energy utilization, AI will connect energy grids with water, building management, and transit systems.
- **Global Energy Trading:** AI forecasting will make it easier to share excess renewable energy globally through cross-border energy markets.
- **AI-Driven Autonomous Grids:** Completely autonomous grids that can predict and adapt to demand surges, weather catastrophes, and infrastructure breakdowns will become commonplace.

Key Takeaway: Renewable energy has a smart, coordinated, and predictive future. AI makes sure that renewable energy is not only produced but also efficiently managed, sent, and integrated worldwide, enabling a resilient, low-carbon energy future.

5.7. Real-Time Modifications: Automated Energy Management That Is Faster and Smarter

Real-time grid optimization is one of AI's most revolutionary contributions to renewable energy. *AI-driven smart grids can react instantly to changes in renewable generation and demand, in contrast to traditional electrical grids that follow defined timetables and frequently need manual intervention or pre-established regulations to modify supply.* As a result, renewable energy is much more dependable, adaptable, and effective.

5.7.1. Energy Storage That Works Automatically

AI makes it possible for smart grids to autonomously store and distribute energy, preventing system instability due to variations in solar and wind generation:

- **Energy Surges:** AI algorithms identify and reroute excess electricity produced by solar panels to battery storage systems, pumped hydro reservoirs, or other storage options when the grid is unable to handle it. This guarantees that no renewable energy is squandered and avoids overburden.

- **Energy Dips**: On the other hand, AI causes the release of stored energy to make up for a reduction in solar production brought on by cloud cover or a slowdown in wind turbines owing to calm conditions, ensuring a constant supply.
- **Predictive Control:** AI can foresee energy spikes or shortages minutes or even hours ahead of time rather than responding after the fact by examining weather forecasts, historical generation patterns, and real-time sensor data. This automated

method increases the overall dependability of renewable energy systems, decreases human intervention, and lowers operational faults.

5.7.2. Dynamic Load Control

AI optimizes demand in addition to managing energy supply to preserve grid stability:

- **Flexible Loads:** AI signals can be used by commercial buildings, water pumps, industrial processes, and electric vehicle charging stations to modify energy usage.
- **Load Shifting:** AI can increase flexible loads to use extra electricity at times of high renewable output. It can lower non-critical demand to avoid blackouts during times of low production.
- **Autonomous Decision-Making**: This technique balances supply and demand throughout the grid in real time without the need for human involvement.

Example: AI systems in smart manufacturing facilities can temporarily halt the operation of non-essential machinery during periods of high demand or move production to times when there is an excess of renewable energy, which lowers costs and stabilizes the grid.

5.7.3. Real-World Example: The Duck Curve in California

The well-known **"Duck Curve"** issue affects **California**'s electrical grid: *midday solar output peaks and then abruptly declines in the late afternoon, causing a sudden spike in demand for conventional power.*

- The state's enormous solar capacity is managed by AI algorithms, which automatically release battery energy that has been saved to support the sharp night-time ramp-up.
- This method eases the shift from solar peak to night-time demand, avoids blackouts, and lessens dependency on gas-fired facilities.
- The end result is a robust, self-correcting grid that can continue to function even in the face of constantly shifting weather patterns and variable renewable energy sources.

5.7.4. **Advantages of Real-Time Adjustments**

a. **Grid Resilience:** Outages and voltage instability are avoided by quick reaction to variations.
b. **Operational Efficiency**: Minimizes energy waste and eliminates the need for fossil fuel backup.
c. **Scalability:** Promotes the use of renewable energy by automatically balancing supply and demand.
d. **Cost Savings**: Reduces operating costs for both utilities and customers by optimizing storage and load control.

Key Takeaway: AI-powered real-time changes transform the historically inflexible electrical grid into an automated, intelligent, and adaptive system that can smoothly integrate intermittent renewable energy sources while preserving stability and effectiveness.

5.8. Managing Various Energy Sources with Hybrid Energy Forecasting

In addition to forecasting the production of a single renewable source, artificial intelligence (AI) makes it possible for hybrid energy forecasting, in which several storage and generation systems are intelligently synchronized to preserve grid stability. This method turns electrical grids into a unified, proactive energy ecosystem rather than a collection of separate, reactive power sources.

5.8.1. Coordination Across Sources

AI's capacity to evaluate several energy sources at once is important to hybrid energy forecasting:

- **Integrated Data Analysis:** AI continuously absorbs and assesses data from battery storage systems, hydro reservoirs, wind turbines, and solar panels.
- **Setting Energy Sources First:** AI determines the energy source to use at any given time based on current and predicted conditions.
- **Example:**
    - AI can instantly release stored hydro or battery energy to sustain grid supply if wind output abruptly decreases due to low wind speeds.
    - In order to prepare for expected night-time demand, AI may choose to store more electricity in batteries during peak solar hours rather than reducing generation.
- **Making Decisions Dynamically**: The grid can react instantly to variations in generation and demand thanks to these

continual, automatic modifications that eliminate the need for human involvement.

Even with a high penetration rate of intermittent renewables, this guarantees dependable, continuous energy supply.

5.8.2. Improving Curtailment and Storage

AI makes sure that energy storage and curtailment are used effectively and strategically, which is essential for managing variability:

- AI predicts when energy will be plentiful and when it will be needed, proactively allocating excess power to storage systems.
- **Minimizing Curtailment**: AI determines the best times and quantities to reduce production, preventing needless losses, rather than wasting extra renewable energy.
- **Balancing Efficiency and Reliability:** AI makes sure that storage is neither overloaded nor underutilized by forecasting both short-term swings and longer-term trends.
- **Example:** To smooth out the load curve and lessen reliance on fossil fuel backup, hybrid networks may use batteries to store extra daytime solar power and release it during night-time peak demand.

5.8.3. Real-World Example: The AI-Powered Hybrid Grid in Europe

A convincing illustration of hybrid energy forecasting in action can be seen in the European electrical grid:

- In order to forecast output and control energy flow across

nations, offshore wind farms, solar parks, and pumped hydro storage are coordinated using AI algorithms.
- This coordination enables utilities to lessen their dependency on gas and coal-fired plants while preserving a steady supply of electricity.
- Despite extremely changeable weather, Europe has been able to maximize renewable use, minimize curtailment, and preserve grid stability by strategically mixing diverse renewable sources and storage systems.

5.8.4. **Grid Transformation**

Forecasting hybrid energy alters our perspective on electrical systems:

a. **From Separate Sources to a Coordinated Ecosystem:** Rather than functioning independently, energy production and storage collaborate dynamically.
b. **Proactive, Not Reactive:** AI plans resources and accounts for unpredictability before imbalances arise.
c. **Greater Renewable Penetration:** Grids can include more solar, wind, and hydro without compromising dependability thanks to coordinated management.

Important Takeaway: AI-powered hybrid energy forecasting synchronizes various storage and generating technologies, resulting in a flexible, intelligent, and resilient grid that can enable a sustainable energy future while reducing waste and reliance on fossil fuels.

5.9. Global Repercussions: Quickening the Decarbonisation Process

Forecasting of renewable energy driven by AI is a strategic driver of global decarbonisation, not only a tool for optimizing the local grid. AI has a direct impact on global climate goals, energy policy, and economic sustainability by facilitating more accurate forecasts and improved integration of renewable energy.

5.9.1. Decreased Fossil Backup: Reducing Carbon Costs and Emissions

Fossil fuel plants have historically been used as a backup in grids with significant renewable penetration to offset the unpredictability of solar and wind power. These inefficient and carbon-intensive facilities are forced to run at partial loads or standby.

This paradigm is altered by AI forecasting:

- Utilities may better schedule renewable dispatch and reduce need on fossil backup by forecasting solar and wind output hours or even days in advance.
- Fuel usage, greenhouse gas emissions, and utility operating costs all decrease with fewer spinning reserves.
- As an illustration, grid managers in Germany have been able to minimize the use of coal-fired power plants during periods of peak renewable production because to AI-based wind and solar forecasting, which has greatly reduced emissions while preserving grid dependability.

5.9.2. A Clean Energy Future Made Possible by Higher Renewable Penetration

The *intermittent nature of solar and wind power* is one of the main obstacles to a grid that is dominated by renewable energy sources. In order to get around this, AI enables grids to incorporate larger proportions of variable energy sources without compromising stability.

- Making it possible to schedule energy storage devices, like pumped hydro or lithium-ion batteries, dynamically so that extra energy can be stored and released as needed.
- Encouraging cross-border renewable trade, which allows excess energy from one area to be predicted and sent to another in anticipation of shortages.

This capacity speeds up the world's renewable energy transition, increasing the likelihood of achieving lofty goals like net-zero emissions by 2050.

5.9.3. Climate Resilience: Assisting Areas at Risk

In addition to being advantageous for developed grids, AI-based forecasting is also essential for areas with erratic weather patterns or inadequate energy infrastructure:

- AI can *anticipate dips or spikes in renewable generation and improve storage and backup systems* beforehand in regions vulnerable to cyclones, droughts, or other extreme weather events.
- By ensuring a more dependable electrical supply, this lessens reliance on imported fossil fuels and promotes investment in renewable infrastructure.

- By more efficiently implementing renewable energy, developing countries may reduce energy poverty and aid in the global decarbonisation process.

5.9.4. Case Study: Forecasting Pilots for Renewable Energy in India

India is now a world leader in the integration of AI-powered renewable energy:

- AI is used by pilot projects to predict wind and solar output over wide, geographically varied areas.
- These projections guarantee that electricity is efficiently provided to the areas that need it most, avoid needless energy curtailment, and lessen dependency on diesel generators.
- By reducing the use of fossil fuels and facilitating a larger proportion of renewable energy in the energy mix, the programs help achieve national decarbonisation goals.

Diagram: Decarbonisation – Integrating Renewables

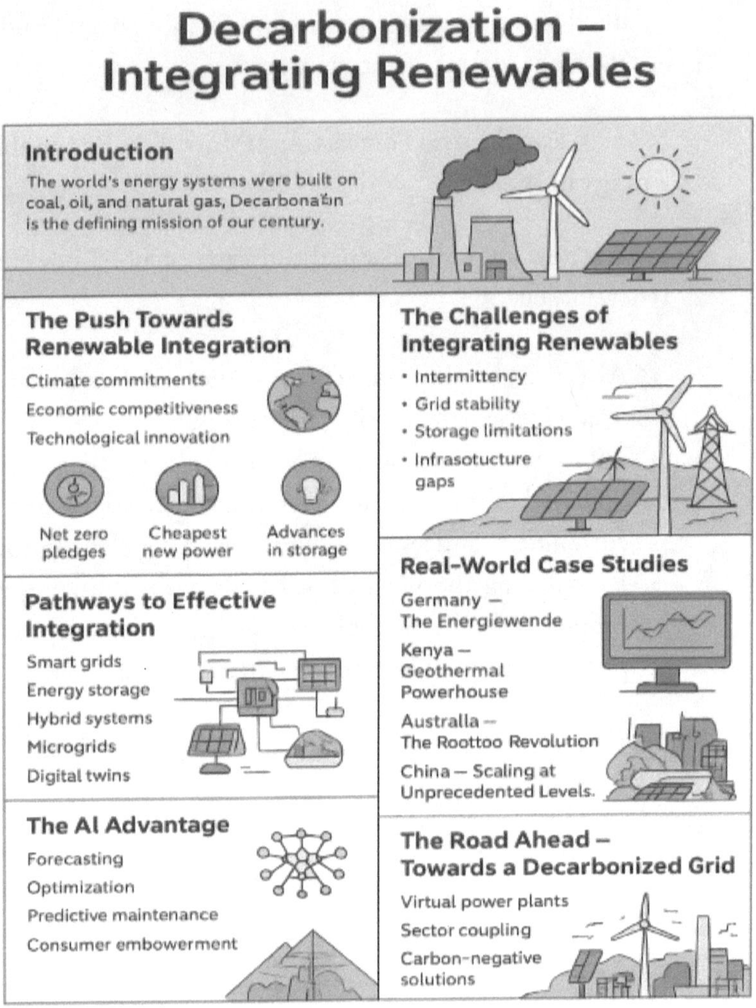

Figure 6: Carbonisation - Integrating Renewables

5.9.5. Important Takeaway

More than just a technical advancement, AI-driven forecasting is a driving force behind the world's low-carbon transition. AI is at the core of the global transition to sustainable, resilient, and decarbonized energy systems by lowering reliance on fossil fuels, allowing grids to handle larger proportions of renewable energy, and improving climate resilience in vulnerable areas.

Chapter 6: AI in Energy Storage Systems

Overview

The foundation of contemporary electrical systems is energy storage. *The development of intermittent renewable energy sources, such as wind and solar, has made intelligent and effective energy storage essential for de-carbonization, cost reduction, and grid dependability.* The design, operation, and maintenance of storage systems are being completely transformed by artificial intelligence (AI). The main ways AI is changing energy storage—from batteries to hydrogen and thermal solutions—are examined in this chapter.

6.1. AI-Driven Predictive Degradation Analysis and Battery Optimization

The foundation of short-term energy storage is batteries, but as they age, their capacity and efficiency decline. AI makes it possible to control battery life more intelligently by:

6.1.1. Predictive Degradation Modelling

Temperature fluctuations, depth of discharge, charging rates, and the chemical aging of battery materials are some of the variables that affect the complicated, nonlinear process of battery degradation. Conventional methods of battery life estimation are based on manufacturer specs or predefined models, which frequently don't account for actual situations.

By using *Machine Learning* (ML) algorithms to examine large datasets from operating batteries, *Artificial Intelligence* (AI) revolutionizes this process through *Predictive Deterioration Modelling*. Important elements consist of:

- **Historical Usage Patterns:** AI looks at the battery's whole operational history, including load fluctuations, inactivity intervals, and the frequency and intensity of cycles of charging and discharging. By doing this, the system can discover which usage patterns hasten deterioration.
- **Environmental Factors:** Variations in humidity and temperature can have a big effect on battery chemistry. Weather and environmental sensor data are included into AI algorithms to forecast how they would affect battery longevity. For example, excessively low temperatures can decrease efficiency, whereas high ambient temperatures can

speed up chemical decomposition.

- **Electrochemical Behaviour Analysis:** To identify minute indications of chemical aging, sophisticated AI systems continuously track voltage curves, internal resistance, and state-of-charge variations.
- **Result:** By integrating these factors, predictive algorithms are able to predict when a battery will lose capacity or perhaps fail, allowing for preventative maintenance or operational modifications.

Example: To anticipate battery health and optimize charging cycles, for instance, **Tesla's Auto-bidirectional Battery Management System (BMS)** uses artificial intelligence. To optimize usable energy and prolong longevity, the system automatically modifies charging rates, restricts excessive use, and rebalances loads across battery modules.

According to Tesla, these solutions enhance overall system dependability and lower unplanned battery failures in both household and grid-scale applications.

6.1.2. Optimizing Charge/Discharge Dynamically

AI can actively control how energy is stored and distributed to *safeguard batteries and maximize economic performance* once prediction models have a better understanding of how batteries deteriorate. Dynamic charge/discharge optimization includes the following steps:

- **Real-Time Grid Coordination:** AI algorithms continuously track energy market pricing, renewable energy production, and power demand. They control discharge during times of high demand or price spikes and modify battery charging during times of abundant supply, such as midday solar peaks.

- **Battery Preservation**: AI can greatly extend battery life by preventing deep discharge or high-rate charging, which hasten wear. To balance short-term energy requirements with long-term health, the AI might, for instance, deliberately discharge only a portion of the battery rather than the entire battery during each high-demand phase.
- **Environmental Responsiveness:** AI can more effectively schedule charging and discharging by taking into account outside variables like predicted temperature, wind patterns, and estimated solar irradiance. For instance, in expectation of lower solar production, the system might hold onto more charge if a gloomy day is forecast.
- **Economic Optimization:** AI makes sure energy is stored or released at the most cost-effective periods, optimizing return on investment, by connecting to energy market pricing or time-of-use tariffs.

Example: In a commercial solar-battery system, AI may discharge the battery during night-time peak hours when energy prices are higher and charge it during periods of high solar output and low electricity prices. This lessens reliance on the grid, saves money, and lessens battery stress.

6.1.3. Case Study: Pacific Gas & Electric (PG&E)

PG&E has been at the forefront of AI applications in utility-scale battery management, showcasing measurable advantages in terms of cost and performance:

- **Implementation**: PG&E used AI-powered analytics on all of its arrays of lithium-ion batteries. Cell voltage, temperature, charge/discharge cycles, and other operating parameters were continually tracked by sensors. Degradation trends were then anticipated by machine learning models before they became serious.

- **Outcomes:** PG&E increased battery lifespan by 15% by proactively modifying maintenance plans, charging rates, and cycle patterns. This is a significant improvement for large-scale installations.
- **Operational Impact:** Unplanned outages were reduced, maintenance expenses were down, and grid flexibility increased. Without sacrificing long-term performance, PG&E was able to optimize battery dispatch for peak shaving and renewable integration thanks to AI.
- **Wider Implications:** This instance shows how AI is a strategic tool that may boost ROI, enhance dependability, and allow utilities to add more intermittent renewable energy to the grid. It is not only a technical advancement.

6.2. Real-time Grid Load Balancing and Storage Matching

Supply and demand must be instantly balanced, which is a basic difficulty for modern electrical grids. Modern grids must incorporate fluctuating renewable sources like solar and wind, whose production can change minute by minute, in contrast to traditional grids, where energy flows were generally predictable. When properly controlled by AI, energy storage serves as the vital buffer, mitigating these fluctuations and guaranteeing grid stability.

6.2.1. Real-Time Load Forecasting

AI-powered real-time load forecasting allows storage systems to predict demand and modify energy delivery instantly. Important elements consist of:

- **Minute-to-Minute Demand Prediction:** AI is able to estimate power demand at incredibly short intervals, often as precise as seconds, using machine learning models based on historical consumption data, weather forecasts, and real-time sensor readings.
- **Proactive Energy Injection or Absorption**: Batteries or other storage systems can pre-charge during times of low demand or strong renewable output and discharge exactly when demand peaks by anticipating the predicted load. This lessens the strain on the grid.
- **Advantages:** Real-time forecasting lowers energy waste, avoids overloading, and lessens dependency on costly, carbon-intensive peaker plants that run on fossil fuels.

Example: A utility-scale AI system can predict that rising temperatures will cause a spike in demand for household air conditioning within the next 15 minutes. This system can then trigger an instantaneous discharge of batteries to fulfil the demand without requiring gas-fired power plants.

6.2.2. Grid Flexibility and Peak Shaving

One crucial way AI-managed storage reduces sharp demand spikes is by peak shaving:

- **During Peak Demand:** AI algorithms coordinate the release of batteries' stored energy during periods of high demand, averting blackouts or voltage decreases. As a result, less costly and frequently polluting peaker plants need to be lit.
- **During Low Demand**: By storing excess renewable energy, like midday solar, rather than reducing it, efficiency can be increased and energy availability guaranteed at the peak of demand.
- **Adaptive Load Management**: AI dynamically balances supply and demand without human intervention by continuously analysing market pricing, weather patterns, and grid conditions to establish the best charging and discharging schedules.

Example: The Hornsdale Power Reserve in South Australia

The **"Tesla Big Battery,"** also known as the **Hornsdale Power Reserve in South Australia,** serves as an example of the practical effects of AI-enabled storage:

- **AI Integration**: Algorithms forecast variations in solar and wind energy production and decide when to release stored energy.

- **Grid Stabilization:** This feature smoothes out irregularities in frequency and voltage by allowing the battery to react in milliseconds to abrupt decreases or surges in generation.
- **Impact**: According to reports, the system has decreased blackout incidents, saved millions of dollars in grid stabilizing expenses, and boosted confidence in the large-scale integration of renewable energy.
- **Significance:** Hornsdale is a prime example of how AI-enabled storage may serve as a modern grid's economic optimizer and rapid-response stabilizer.

6.2.3. Microgrids with AI Optimization

AI-driven storage has the potential to transform localized or microgrid systems, such as campuses, small towns, or industrial complexes, in addition to utility-scale grids:

- **Real-Time Generation and Consumption Matching:** AI keeps an eye on local solar, wind, battery, and energy consumption to make sure that generation is either used effectively or stored for later.
- **Cost and Carbon Optimization:** Microgrids can limit grid dependency, lower power costs, and reduce carbon emissions by strategically storing renewable energy for times of peak demand.
- **Autonomous Operation:** Without human supervision, AI can balance load, ensure dependability, and stop outages in remote or off-grid locations.

Example: Industrial locations that use a lot of on-site solar energy and AI-optimized storage can lower peak electricity costs by 20–30%, showing both economic and environmental advantages.

6.2.4. Key Takeaways:

AI enables storage systems to function as a clever middleman, instantly adjusting supply and demand.

- Dynamic dispatch and predictive forecasting enhance renewable integration, save costs, and avoid blackouts.
- From massive projects like Hornsdale to microgrids in isolated towns, AI-driven storage guarantees the economical, sustainable, and efficient use of energy.

6.3. The Role of AI's in Next-Gen Thermal and Hydrogen Storage Systems

Although *lithium-ion batteries remain the industry standard for short-term energy storage, newer technologies like thermal storage and hydrogen are essential for large-scale, industrial, and long-duration energy applications.* AI is essential to maximizing these systems' potential since it allows for precise control, optimization, and grid integration.

6.3.1. Storage of Hydrogen

A growing number of people believe that hydrogen is a flexible energy source that can store extra renewable energy for days, weeks, or even months. However, because of intermittent renewable energy and changing grid demand, effectively coordinating hydrogen production, compression, storage, and utilization is extremely complex. AI tackles these issues by:

- **Optimal Electrolysis Scheduling:** To identify the best times to operate water electrolysis units, machine learning algorithms examine current solar and wind output, power costs, and anticipated demand. This maximizes hydrogen yield while lowering energy expenses.
- **Compression and Storage Management:** Energy is used when storing hydrogen because it needs to be compressed or liquefied. AI can minimize energy waste by optimizing storage usage and compression schedules.
- **Fuel Cell Dispatch Optimization:** AI forecasts the best dispatch time to satisfy peak demand, maintain grid stability, or effectively feed industrial operations when hydrogen is

transformed back into electricity using fuel cells.

Example: In hybrid renewable-hydrogen systems, artificial intelligence (AI) makes sure that solar energy is used for electrolysis during the day while hydrogen reserves supply power at night or at times when renewable output is low, optimizing system efficiency and financial return.

6.3.2. Thermal Storage

Energy can be stored in thermal storage systems as either heat or cold, which can then be used for heating and cooling or transformed into electricity.

- **Predictive Charge and Discharge Management**: AI models predict demand for electricity, heating, or cooling, dynamically regulating when to release or store thermal energy. This is one way AI improves their performance.
- **Reducing Energy Losses:** Insulation losses and inefficient energy conversion are common problems with thermal storage. AI keeps an eye on environmental factors and system performance to minimize these losses.
- **Operational Cost Optimization:** AI makes sure that stored energy is used when it is most cost-effective by coordinating thermal storage utilization with fluctuating energy prices and renewable generation.
- **Example of Technologies**:
    - **Molten Salt Storage:** In *Concentrated Solar Power* (CSP) plants, molten salt storage is used to store heat for use in producing electricity after sunset.
    - **Ice Storage:** Commercial buildings use ice storage to store cooling energy overnight when electricity is less expensive and release it during peak hours during the

day.

6.3.3. Hybrid Systems That Are Integrated

Multi-layered energy storage ecosystems that integrate several storage technologies for optimum performance are made possible by AI:

- **Short-Term vs. Long-Term Storage**: Hydrogen stores energy for extended periods of time, whereas batteries manage quick swings and brief peaks. Industrial operations and heating/cooling are supported by thermal storage.
- **Dynamic Coordination:** AI systems plan the cycles of charging and discharging for all forms of storage according to current grid conditions, predictions for renewable energy, and changes in the power market.
- **Resilience and Cost Efficiency**: Hybrid systems enhance energy security, decrease operating costs, and lessen dependency on fossil fuels by combining various storage options.

6.3.4. Case Study Japan's Hydrogen Strategy:

Japan is leading the way in the use of AI-driven hydrogen storage to balance variable renewable energy on a large scale:

- **Integration with Renewables:** To create a flexible energy ecology, Japanese utilities integrate thermal, wind, and solar generation with hydrogen storage.
- **AI-Driven Optimization**: The best time to produce, store, and convert hydrogen back into power is decided by algorithms. Real-time electricity costs, weather patterns, and changing energy supplies are all taken into account by the

system.

- **Impact:** AI optimization lowers energy waste, guarantees a steady supply during times when renewable output is low, and boosts the grid's overall efficiency.
- **Significance**: This illustrates how artificial intelligence (AI) is crucial for providing long-duration storage solutions and incorporating them into intricate energy systems that rely heavily on renewable sources.

6.3.5. Important Takeaways:

- For industrial applications and long-term energy balancing, thermal and hydro storage are crucial.
- AI coordinates various storage types for maximum efficiency, minimizes losses, and forecasts ideal operating schedules.
- AI-powered integrated hybrid systems build low-carbon, resilient, and economical energy infrastructures.
- AI's revolutionary potential in next-generation storage systems is demonstrated by real-world implementations, such as Japan's hydrogen strategy.
- AI optimizes charge/discharge cycles, forecasts degradation, and prolongs battery life.
- AI-driven storage management in real time lowers costs and improves grid stability.
- AI is crucial for developing storage technologies that enable resilient and integrated energy ecosystems, such as thermal and hydrogen systems.

Chapter 7: AI-Powered Peer-to-Peer Energy Trading and Decentralized Grids

Overview

The power grid is changing from a top-down, centralized structure to a flexible, decentralized one. *Distributed Energy Resources* (DERs) like wind turbines, rooftop solar, and home energy storage have made consumers more than simply passive consumers; they are now *Prosumers* who *can generate, store, and even trade energy*. At the core of this change are blockchain and artificial intelligence (AI) technologies, which make energy markets more intelligent, transparent, and highly automated.

7.1. A Combination of Blockchain and AI for Decentralized Energy Markets

Energy transactions can be recorded in a transparent and safe ledger thanks to blockchain technology. When paired with AI, it revolutionizes energy trading:

a. **Smart Contracts:** AI can use blockchain-based smart contracts to autonomously initiate energy exchanges, estimate demand, and assess market circumstances. Without human assistance, a house battery, for example, can sell extra energy to a neighbour at the best market price.
b. **Fraud Prevention and Transparency**: AI identifies irregularities like phony bids, underreported production, or unusual consumption habits, while blockchain guarantees that every transaction is unchangeable.
c. **Dynamic Pricing**: AI models determine fair, dynamic pricing for peer-to-peer (P2P) energy trading by analysing supply, demand, and weather trends in real time. Communities can use local renewable energy more effectively and save money.
d. **Case Study: The Brooklyn Microgrid initiative in Brooklyn**, New York, enables local solar energy trading by utilizing blockchain technology and artificial intelligence. Blockchain guarantees safe transaction settlement, while AI forecasts energy surplus and optimizes trade timing.

7.1.1. Smart Contracts

Encoded on a blockchain, *smart contracts are self-executing agreements whose terms are automatically enforced without the need for human intervention.* Smart contracts become extremely clever and adaptive when combined with AI:

- **Predictive Execution:** AI systems keep a close eye on weather forecasts, grid load, and market circumstances. Smart contracts can determine the optimal moment to buy or sell energy based on this data. For instance, the smart contract can automatically plan sales to a neighbour or local microgrid at the most profitable price if a home solar battery is predicted to produce excess electricity at noon.
- **Automatic Energy Trading:** Businesses and households no longer have to manually arrange trades or keep an eye on the energy markets all the time. Smart contracts and AI predictions work together to provide smooth, automated trade while guaranteeing the best possible use of dispersed energy resources.
- **Scalability:** Large-scale *Peer-to-Peer* (P2P) energy markets are made possible by smart contracts' ability to handle thousands of concurrent transactions across numerous homes, microgrids, or VPPs without human intervention.
- **Example:** A house equipped with a battery storage system can sell extra solar energy to a neighbour who is in greater need. While the smart contract carries out the sale promptly and transparently, AI determines the best quantity to sell and the best time to do so in order to maximize profit.

7.1.2. Prevention of Fraud and Openness

Every transaction in decentralized energy markets is documented on a blockchain, resulting in an unchangeable and impenetrable ledger. AI actively looks for anomalies to improve security and trust:

- **Anomaly Detection:** AI systems are able to identify odd trends in energy use or output, such as abrupt increases, persistent underreporting, or attempts to influence market prices. These irregularities cause automated rejection of questionable transactions or alerts for additional verification.

- **Immutable Audit Trails:** Blockchain makes sure that all energy transactions, no matter how small, are permanently recorded, preventing energy credits from being double-spent or production data from being falsified.
- **Trustless Transactions:** Prosumers can trade energy with confidence because the blockchain ledger verifies authenticity, and AI protects the system from manipulation.
- **Example:** If a prosumer tries to sell energy they haven't generated, AI recognizes the discrepancy in production data versus historical patterns and flags the transaction automatically, preventing fraud before it can impact the market.

7.1.3. **Dynamic Pricing**

Conventional energy price is fixed and frequently unrelated to current supply and demand. Fair, effective, and responsive pricing is made possible in P2P energy markets by AI-driven dynamic pricing:

- **Real-Time Market Analysis**: To make real-time price adjustments, AI continuously examines local supply (solar, wind, storage) and demand (home use, EV charging, nearby enterprises).
- **Weather-Responsive Adjustments**: Price optimization takes into account predicted weather conditions, such as sunny or windy spells. For example, local costs may rise during a foggy period, but they may fall during an anticipated spike in solar power.
- **Community-Level Optimization:** AI makes sure that prices take into account the needs of both individuals and

neighbourhoods, promoting energy sharing where it makes sense and avoiding energy waste.

- **Cost and Carbon Savings:** By encouraging the use of locally produced renewable energy instead of grid electricity, dynamic pricing lowers consumer costs and carbon emissions.
- **Example:** AI forecasts surplus solar output between 11 AM and 2 PM in a community with plenty of sunlight. During this window, prices are dynamically reduced to incentivize neighbours to purchase excess energy. On the other hand, AI raises rates during evening demand peaks, indicating a need for microgrids or residential batteries to store energy.

7.1.4. Real-Time Market Analysis

AI makes it possible for energy markets to function dynamically by continuously evaluating local supply and demand data:

- **Granular Supply Monitoring**: AI monitors the energy produced locally by *Distributed Energy Resources* (DERs), such as solar panels, wind turbines, and household batteries. It has the ability to instantly identify variations, shortages, and surpluses.
- **Demand Forecasting:** AI forecasts peak demand periods and modifies energy flows in accordance with them by tracking local company usage, EV charging schedules, and household consumption trends.
- **Making Decisions Dynamically**: AI can automatically modify energy pricing, distribute extra energy to regions with high demand, or store it in batteries for later use thanks to real-time insights. In addition to preventing local blackouts or grid pressure, this guarantees effective market operation.
- **Example**: AI observes that three residences are charging

electric cars at the same time in a residential microgrid, while solar output decreases as a result of passing clouds. In order to prevent overload, prices are automatically raised to prioritize vital energy consumption and limit demand.

7.1.5. Weather-Responsive Adjustments

Weather has a big impact on the production of renewable energy. AI optimizes energy pricing and delivery by combining current and predicted meteorological data:

- **Predictive Generation Modelling:** AI predicts energy production by taking into account weather conditions such as wind speed and anticipated sunlight.
- **Price Adaptation:** Market prices are lowered if sunny or windy weather is predicted because of the expected energy excess. On the other hand, calm or overcast days raise prices to reflect the lack of supply.
- **Supply-Demand Balancing:** AI encourages customers to shift usage to times when renewable energy is abundant by proactively modifying rates based on weather, increasing overall efficiency.

Example: AI forecasts a solar surplus on a particularly sunny afternoon and lowers local electricity costs, encouraging surrounding companies to plan high-energy activities like manufacturing or laundry for this window.

7.1.6. Optimization at the Community Level

AI makes sure that pricing and energy distribution benefit the entire community, not just individuals:

- **Neighbourhood Coordination:** To cut down on energy waste and lessen dependency on the main grid, AI balances supply and demand across homes, businesses, and microgrids.
- **Promoting Energy Sharing**: Peer-to-peer trade can be encouraged by automatically pricing excess energy from one household at a price that is appealing to surrounding neighbours.
- **Adaptive Pricing Policies**: AI takes into account both local limitations and group objectives, such increasing the use of renewable energy sources, cutting expenses, or decreasing system congestion.
- **Example**: AI detects, that one residence in a nearby microgrid has extra solar electricity while another has high evening demand. The neighbourhood energy balance is maintained by the system automatically offering a favourable price to promote energy transfer.

7.1.7. Savings on Cost and Carbon

AI-powered dynamic pricing directly encourages sustainable energy use, reducing expenses and their negative effects on the environment:

- **Reduced Grid Dependence:** AI lessens the need for electricity from fossil fuel-based power plants by promoting the use of locally produced renewable energy.
- **Optimized Consumption Patterns**: When renewable generation is high, consumers can move high-energy activities to times when prices are low.
- **Reduction of Carbon Footprint:** Using local renewable energy sources more effectively than conventional grid electricity reduces greenhouse gas emissions and helps achieve climate goals.

Example: When there is excess solar energy available locally, a smart AI system alerts a family to turn on EV chargers and washing machines, lowering the carbon footprint of the household and its dependency on fossil fuel electricity.

When combined, these AI-driven tactics produce an energy ecosystem that is incredibly flexible, effective, and sustainable. The system runs more smoothly, communities profit monetarily, and the use of renewable energy sources is maximized.

A self-regulating, transparent, and effective P2P energy marketplace is produced by combining smart contracts, AI-driven fraud detection, and dynamic pricing. This empowers prosumers and fortifies the decentralized grid.

7.2. Virtual Power Plants (VPPs) and Microgrids

Small, regional energy networks known as *Microgrids* can function both separately and in tandem with the larger grid. They offer grid-scale flexibility without exclusively depending on big power plants when paired with artificial intelligence (AI) and consolidated into *Virtual Power Plants* (VPPs):

- **AI Optimization:** To balance local supply and demand, AI forecasts energy generation from dispersed sources and plans storage dispatch.
- **Grid Resilience:** Microgrids can cut off from the main grid in an emergency, ensuring that vital infrastructure always has power.
- **Scalable Energy Aggregation:** VPPs serve as a single controllable entity that takes part in wholesale energy markets by combining several microgrids, household batteries, and renewable generators.

Example: Siemens and **Next Kraftwerke** have established VPPs in Germany that combine thousands of small-scale renewable energy producers and use artificial intelligence (AI) to predict output and effectively bid into energy markets.

7.2.1. AI Optimisation

By anticipating generation and controlling energy flows, artificial intelligence revolutionizes the operation of *Microgrids* and *Distributed Energy Resources* (DERs):

- **Predictive Generation:** Using historical data, weather

forecasts, and real-time sensor inputs, AI models predict the energy output from solar panels, wind turbines, and other renewable sources. This makes it possible to precisely predict changes in supply.

- **Smart Storage Dispatch:** AI controls batteries and other storage devices to store extra energy during times of high generation and release it during times of peak demand. This guarantees that energy will always be available when and where it is required.
- **Load Balancing:** AI constantly tracks generating levels and consumption trends to maximize energy distribution throughout the microgrid, cutting down on waste and averting local shortages.

Example: AI forecasts a cloudy afternoon in a community that uses solar power. In order to ensure that residences have electricity even in the event of a fall in solar output, it uses excess morning solar energy to pre-charge batteries.

Diagram: AI Optimisation across Energy Sources

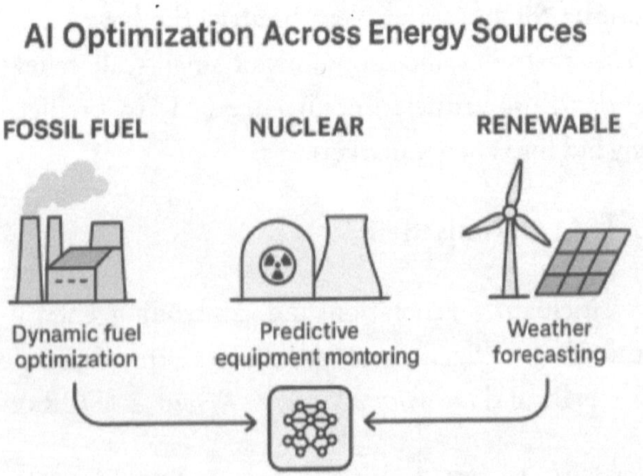

Figure 7: AI Optimisation across Energy Sources

7.2.2. Grid Resilience

Energy resilience is improved by microgrids, especially in times of emergency or grid failure:

- **Island Mode Operation:** During blackouts or severe weather, microgrids can cut off from the main grid to keep vital infrastructure like data centres, hospitals, and emergency services powered.
- **Autonomous Energy Management:** AI in microgrids dynamically modifies demand, storage, and generation priorities to maintain the proper operation of critical systems.
- **Quick Recovery:** Microgrids can easily re-join to the main grid once it stabilizes, reducing downtime and interruptions to operations.

Example: A hospital microgrid that is powered by a combination of solar panels and stored battery energy can continue to function independently during a storm that disrupts the central grid. To increase energy availability, AI determines which systems can function at lower loads and which run at maximum capacity.

7.2.3. Aggregation of Scalable Energy

Virtual Power Plants (VPPs) combine several dispersed energy sources and microgrids to function as a single, controllable entity:

- **Centralized Coordination, Distributed Resources**: AI treats several microgrids, batteries, and renewable energy sources as a single virtual power plant that may take part in wholesale markets by coordinating energy output, storage, and consumption across these systems.

- **Market Participation**: By selling stored or excess energy at peak pricing, VPPs can maximize revenue streams, bid into energy markets, and offer auxiliary services like frequency regulation.
- **Scalable Flexibility:** VPPs can match the operational capacity of conventional power plants without leaving an environmental impact by integrating many small-scale resources.

Example: Next Kraftwerke oversees a VPP of thousands of wind, solar, and biogas units in Germany. AI uses dispersed resources to provide grid-scale reliability by predicting output, coordinating storage, and optimizing energy bids in the wholesale market.

Scalable VPPs, resilient microgrids, and AI optimization work together to create a decentralized grid that is reliable, adaptable, and efficient. Even during extreme events, this architecture maintains dependable power delivery while enabling communities and utilities to more efficiently exploit renewable energy.

7.3. Enabling Customers to Become "Prosumers"

The emergence of *Prosumers*, or *families or enterprises that generate, use, and sell energy,* is one of the most revolutionary effects of decentralized grids:

- **Residential Solar + Storage:** AI forecasts solar output and household energy usage, allowing for the best timing for selling or storing excess energy.
- **P2P Energy Trading Platforms**: These AI and blockchain-powered platforms let prosumers trade locally with VPPs or their neighbours. Prices change on the fly according to local supply and demand.
- **Promoting Renewable Adoption:** By making money off of surplus energy, prosumers are incentivized to purchase energy-efficient appliances, solar panels, and batteries.

Example: Homes in Australia can sell extra solar energy to nearby companies or neighbours using the Power Ledger platform. AI systems maximize profits while preserving grid stability by optimizing trading schedules and price offers.

7.3.1. Solar + Storage for Homes

By cleverly controlling energy production and consumption, *Artificial Intelligence* (AI) raises the value of household solar and storage systems:

- **Predictive Consumption Modelling:** AI tracks how much energy is used by appliances, air conditioning and heating systems, and EV charging in homes. It can plan solar or battery discharges to optimize efficiency by predicting demand.

- **Optimized Solar Utilization:** Using previous sunlight data and weather projections, AI forecasts solar energy generation. It decides whether energy should be used right now, stored for later, or sold to nearby residents or the local grid.
- **Cost and Efficiency Benefits:** When grid rates are high, homeowners can use solar or stored energy to save money, and they can sell excess energy during periods of high demand to optimize profits.

Example: By using AI to store extra morning solar power and sell it in the early evening when local demand increases, a household with rooftop solar and a home battery can generate revenue while lowering their dependency on the grid.

7.3.2. Platforms for P2P Energy Trading

Blockchain and artificial intelligence are used by peer-to-peer energy trading platforms to provide safe, easy, and dynamic energy transactions amongst prosumers:

- **Automated Market Matching**: AI continuously pairs energy buyers and sellers, optimizing quantities and pricing according to supply, demand, and anticipated consumption trends.
- **Secure Transactions**: Blockchain guarantees that every transaction is visible and unchangeable, fostering confidence in decentralized energy exchanges.
- **Integration with VPPs:** By linking prosumers to bigger virtual power plants, P2P platforms enable aggregated energy to take part in wholesale markets while maintaining the flexibility of local trade.
- **Dynamic Pricing:** When renewable resources are plentiful,

prices are dynamically adjusted based on local generation and consumption, encouraging the use of energy.

Example: Using a blockchain-enabled platform, a home in a suburban microgrid can sell extra solar energy to a neighbour. Using projected solar output, household consumption, and community demand, AI determines the best trade price, and smart contracts automatically complete the deal.

7.3.3. Promoting the Adoption of Renewable Energy

Prosumers are given financial incentives to embrace green energy technology by decentralized grids and AI-powered trading platforms:

- **Monetizing Extra Energy:** By selling extra energy instead of letting it go unused, homeowners can generate income, which increases the appeal of solar panel and storage investments.
- **Promoting Energy Efficiency:** To lower consumption expenses and increase trade profits, AI can suggest energy-efficient appliances and the best times to use them.
- **Impact at the Community Level**: Local renewable penetration rises as more homes become prosumers, decreasing dependency on fossil fuels and boosting grid resilience.

Example: A small company joins a local P2P trading network and installs solar panels. It encourages other local businesses to use similar renewable solutions and more quickly offsets installation costs by selling excess energy during times of peak demand.

When combined, home solar, smart storage, AI-powered peer-to-peer trading, and financial incentives enable consumers to take an active role in the energy ecosystem, transforming conventional energy users into prosumers and promoting a sustainable, decentralized grid.

7.4. Obstacles and the Path Ahead

The decentralized grid has drawbacks even though it promises efficiency and user empowerment:

- **Risks to Cybersecurity:** Strong AI-driven security monitoring is required since more nodes and transactions make a system more susceptible to cyberattacks.
- **Frameworks for Regulation**: Policies that permit peer-to-peer trade, safeguard consumers, and incorporate decentralized energy into the larger grid must be developed by governments.
- **Scalability and Interoperability**: For broad adoption, it is essential to guarantee that various blockchain platforms, VPPs, and microgrids can cooperate seamlessly.

Notwithstanding these challenges, decentralized grids driven by blockchain and artificial intelligence (AI) are the energy of the future: robust, effective, and democratically governed. *By converting consumers into engaged members of the energy ecosystem, they make the grid more resilient and sustainable.*

7.4.1. Cybersecurity Risks

New cybersecurity issues are brought forth by the exponential growth in connected devices, prosumers, and transactions that occurs as energy systems become decentralized:

- **Increased Attack Surface**: Every home battery, solar inverter, microgrid, smart meter, and VPP is a possible point of entry for hackers. Market prices can be manipulated or energy flow disrupted by compromising even one node.

- **AI-Driven Security Monitoring:** To identify irregularities or questionable activity instantly, sophisticated AI continuously scans network traffic, energy flows, and transaction patterns. Machine learning models have the ability to recognize intrusions, including ransomware attempts, data manipulation, and unauthorized access, and initiate automatic defences.
- **Resilience and Recovery**: In order to avoid blackouts or monetary losses, AI may also model attack scenarios and plan countermeasures, such as separating compromised nodes, rerouting energy flows, and promptly returning to normal operations.

Example: AI in a VPP can identify odd bid patterns that point to a cyberattack to influence regional energy prices. To avoid a possible market disturbance, the system automatically flags the behaviour, isolates the impacted nodes, and notifies operators.

7.4.2. **Regulatory Structures**

Clear, encouraging, and flexible regulations are essential to the development of *Decentralized Grids* and *Peer-to-Peer* (P2P) energy trading:

- **P2P Trading Law:** Governments must enact laws that let prosumers to sell energy to neighbours or VPPs directly without going against market laws or utility monopolies.
- **Protection of Consumers**: Regulations must guarantee openness, reasonable prices, and defense against deception, data breaches, and unfair market manipulation.
- **Grid Integration Standards**: In order to safely and

dependably integrate decentralized energy resources to the main grid, regulators must establish technical standards that cover data interchange, energy quality, and emergency procedures.

- **Incentives and Subsidies:** To promote the growth of renewable energy sources and grid resilience, governments might hasten adoption by offering financial incentives for prosumers, microgrids, or VPP participation.

Example: Families in **Australia** are now able to lawfully sell solar energy through P2P platforms while upholding safety and transparency standards because to regulatory changes made in states like Victoria and New South Wales.

7.4.3. Interoperability and Scalability

Decentralized energy systems require seamless collaboration between multiple platforms, networks, and technologies in order to operate effectively at scale:

- **Cross-Platform Integration:** Blockchain-based trading platforms, VPPs, and microgrids frequently employ disparate software and communication protocols. Data interchange, coordinated energy dispatch, and unified market participation are all made possible by interoperability.
- **Modular Scalability:** Without causing performance deterioration or complexity bottlenecks, systems must enable gradual expansion from a small number of families to thousands of prosumers.
- **Standardized Protocols:** Diverse platforms and devices can work together by establishing open standards for communication, transaction verification, and energy metering.

- **Potential for Global Collaboration:** Interoperable systems make it easier to trade energy across borders or even within regions, which improves the use of renewable energy sources and market efficiency on a broader scale.

To enable coordinated P2P energy trading while maintaining system stability, European projects such as the **Transactive Energy Europe** initiative *concentrate on integrating different microgrids and VPPs across nations using standardized protocols.*

For decentralized energy markets to grow safely, effectively, and scalable, cybersecurity, regulatory compliance, and interoperability must all be addressed simultaneously. Even the most sophisticated blockchain and AI technologies cannot reach their full potential without these pillars.

Chapter 8: AI-Powered Grid Cybersecurity

Overview

Unprecedented efficiency, flexibility, and dependability are brought about by the modernization of electrical grids using AI and smart technology. However, new cybersecurity issues are also brought about by this digital transition. Grids driven by AI are more vulnerable to advanced cyberattacks and more resilient to conventional assaults.

AI improves grid security by making it possible for:

- **Detecting Threats In Real Time:** When grid activities are continuously monitored, anomalies, incursions, or odd patterns are found before they become more serious.
- **Predictive Defense**: By using machine learning to foresee possible weaknesses, at-risk components can be isolated in advance.
- **Automated Reactions**: During attacks, intelligent systems are able to isolate impacted segments, swiftly reroute power flows, and preserve stability.

  However, AI also creates vulnerabilities:

8.1. Targeted AI Model Attacks

Machine learning models are used by AI-driven grids to make decisions in real time, such forecasting demand, identifying irregularities, or maximizing electricity flows. However, these models can be purposefully altered:

- **Data Poisoning:** Malicious data can be introduced into AI training datasets by attackers. Falsified readings from IoT sensors, for instance, might teach the AI to mistakenly see regular activities as abnormal, or vice versa, which could lead to needless shutdowns or leave vulnerabilities unfixed.

- **Model Evasion:** Without setting off alarms, hackers can carefully create inputs that deceive AI models. The AI may be tricked into underestimating load stress by minute changes in sensor signals, for example, increasing the risk of overloads or equipment damage.
- **Consequences:** In AI-managed grids, even small errors in prediction can have a cascading effect, resulting in incorrect automated reactions, delayed threat detection, or power misallocation, which can cause equipment failures or outages.

8.2. Increased Areas of Attack

The contemporary AI-powered grid integrates a wide range of devices and is extensively networked:

- **Smart meters with IoT sensors**: Attackers could potentially enter through any sensor sending data over networks. Unauthorized access to grid controllers or erroneous consumption data could be transmitted via compromised meters.

- **Distributed Energy Resources (DERs) and Autonomous Controllers**: AI-powered controllers that can independently modify storage and generation are desirable targets. By altering local energy flows, a corrupted controller might cause the larger network to become unstable.
- **Supply Chain Vulnerabilities**: Additional risks are introduced by third-party services, cloud-based AI platforms, and hardware or software updates. The AI systems of the grid may be indirectly compromised by attackers aiming for these components.

8.3. Quick Error Propagation

AI-managed networks, in contrast to conventional grids, make automatic judgments that are carried out nearly instantly:

- **Error Amplification**: If an AI misclassifies a threat or decides to operate incorrectly, the automated system may apply this error to several nodes at once, increasing the severity of the problem.
- **Cascade Failures**: For instance, an AI might inadvertently overload another area of the grid by diverting electricity away from a perceived threat. In just a few minutes, such cascading effects might result in widespread disruptions.
- **Self-Reinforcing Loops**: AI feedback loops can be abused by adversaries; an initial anomaly may set off AI-driven corrective actions that inadvertently make matters worse, setting off a swift chain reaction across the system.

These flaws collectively show that, despite its strength, AI poses difficult cybersecurity problems. In addition to protecting networked and physical equipment, safeguarding AI-powered grids necessitates maintaining the integrity of the AI models themselves, as well as ongoing monitoring and human supervision.

Case studies show how AI-driven cybersecurity is essential for preserving operational integrity, averting blackouts, and guaranteeing energy security. One example is Europe's defense against state-sponsored assaults on smart grids.

Essentially, cybersecurity in AI-powered grids involves striking a balance between protecting the grid by utilizing AI's speed and intelligence and preventing the very systems that depend on AI from becoming targets themselves.

The interaction between increased efficiency and new cybersecurity threats becomes crucial as electric grids develop into AI-powered, self-governing systems. AI creates new attack surfaces that adversaries can take advantage of, even though it provides previously unheard-of capabilities for threat detection and response.

8.3. AI as a Vulnerability and a Protector

Grid cybersecurity is altered by AI in two ways:

- **Making the Grid Stronger**:
    - AI systems are able to continuously monitor millions of data points, spotting odd trends that could point to ransomware attacks, equipment tampering, or penetration.
    - Pre-emptive measures, including rerouting power flows or isolating susceptible nodes, are made possible by predictive analytics before an attack has a chance to spread throughout the network.
- **Presenting New Risks:**
    - Attackers may contaminate training data to produce blind spots or alter the grid's reaction logic, making AI models themselves targets. If compromised, automated systems could spread mistakes more quickly than people can respond.
    - The attack surface of smart grids is increased by interconnected equipment, such as autonomous controllers and Internet of Things sensors.

8.4. Real-Time Threat Detection

Modern cybersecurity solutions rely heavily on AI's capacity to evaluate large, complicated data streams:

- **Anomaly Detection**: AI systems are able to identify deviations immediately after learning typical operating patterns. Alerts are triggered, for instance, by unexpected control commands, aberrant access requests, or odd voltage fluctuations.
- **Deep Learning Models**: Neural networks are able to detect minute correlations that conventional rule-based systems are unable to detect, including coordinated attacks involving several substations or anomalies across the grid.
- **Automated Response**: To reduce downtime and stop cascading failures, certain systems have the ability to automatically separate compromised segments.

8.4. Case Study: Safeguarding Smart Grids in Europe

State-sponsored cyberattacks have targeted Europe as a result of its shift to smart grids. In order to protect these systems, AI-driven cybersecurity solutions have been essential:

- In 2022, coordinated infiltration attempts targeting several grid substations were discovered by a German AI-based monitoring technology. The system prevented extensive outages by automatically quarantining impacted segments based on real-time analysis of network traffic and operational irregularities.
- AI tools regularly evaluate vulnerabilities in historical systems integrated with contemporary smart grids throughout the European Union, pointing out weak points and suggesting improvements to authentication procedures, access controls, and encryption.
- Before an actual assault happens, cybersecurity professionals may improve incident response strategies and predict attack scenarios with AI-powered simulations.

8.5. The Way Ahead

1. Human-AI Hybrid Security

AI is excellent at identifying anomalies, digesting enormous amounts of grid data in real time, and carrying out quick automated reactions. But human knowledge is still essential:

- **Strategic Interpretation**: While AI can identify possible dangers, humans are still required to decipher complicated or unclear situations, such as differentiating between a planned hack and a normal system fluctuation.
- **Ethical and Legal Oversight**: AI decisions, such as cutting off operations or isolating a grid piece, can have a big societal and economic impact. Humans make sure that these behaviours adhere to moral and legal requirements.
- **Incident Response Coordination**: While AI concentrates on containment and mitigation, humans organize multifaceted responses, including communicating with law enforcement, regulators, and adjacent grids.

Example: Artificial intelligence (AI) technologies in real-world European smart grids immediately isolate suspect nodes, but human engineers determine if the anomaly is a coordinated state-sponsored attack or a false positive.

1. Sturdy AI Architecture

AI must be built to foresee and resist hostile strategies in order to protect grids:

- **Resilience to Data Poisoning:** To stop hostile inputs from changing the AI's behaviour, training data must be regularly checked. Integrity is preserved through methods like data redundancy and anomaly-resistant learning.

- **Defense against Evasion Attacks:** AI models must use techniques like ensemble models, adversarial training, and continuous retraining with real-time feedback to identify inputs that are specifically designed to evade detection.
- **Explainable AI (XAI):** By enabling operators to comprehend the rationale behind certain predictions or actions, transparent AI models lower the possibility of misunderstandings and uphold user confidence in automated systems.
- **Continuous Stress Testing**: AI algorithms are improved through penetration testing and attack scenario simulations, which strengthens them against unanticipated threats.

1. **International Cooperation**

In AI-powered grids, cyber threats are rarely local; instead, they can travel across borders and take advantage of supply chains and interconnected infrastructures:

- **Threat Intelligence Sharing:** To increase situational awareness, operators and governments share real-time information on threats, attack trends, and threat actors.
- **Coordinated Incident Response**: To prevent a cyberattack in one nation from spreading to nearby grids, regional or global coordination is necessary. Predictive analytics for possible cross-border effects is one way AI can help.
- **Best Practices and Standardization:** To ensure that AI-driven grids around the world adhere to strong defensive measures, collaborative frameworks like the U.S. CISA guidelines and the EU's NIS2 Directive help standardize AI security regulations.

Example: After coordinated ransomware assaults on European energy suppliers, several nations were able to prevent outages and pre-emptively safeguard susceptible substations by sharing AI-driven insights.

In order to protect against complex, quickly changing cyber threats, these tactics demonstrate that safeguarding AI-powered grids necessitates a synergy between AI capabilities, human skills, and international cooperation.

AI in smart grids has two sides: it strengthens existing weaknesses while also introducing new ones. To guarantee resilient and dependable power distribution, success requires fusing cutting-edge AI capabilities with strong cybersecurity procedures, ongoing monitoring, and cross-border cooperation.

Chapter 9: AI for Climate-Resilient Energy Systems

Overview:

Extreme weather events, protracted droughts, heatwaves, and rising sea levels are all becoming more dangerous for energy systems as climate change accelerates. Because they were designed for earlier times, traditional energy infrastructures find it difficult to remain dependable and effective in the face of current demands. AI makes predictive, adaptive, and resilient energy management possible, which is a revolutionary approach.

Important Functions of AI in Climate Resilience:

a. **Predictive Disaster Response**: Before disasters occur, AI models foresee outages and infrastructure risks by analysing historical and real-time meteorological, grid, and environmental data.
b. **Adaptive Energy Management:** AI may dynamically modify generation and storage by integrating diverse energy sources, making up for disturbances such as decreased solar efficiency during storms or droughts that impact hydropower.
c. **Infrastructure Planning and Optimization:** Resilient grid design, microgrid deployment, and equipment maintenance schedules are guided by machine learning algorithms that assess climate risks over decades.
d. **Quick Recovery and Resource Allocation:** AI minimizes downtime for vital services in post-disaster scenarios by optimizing personnel deployment, repair prioritizing, and energy redistribution.

Result: AI turns energy systems from reactive and inflexible networks into intelligent, flexible grids that can lower carbon emissions, maintain a steady supply of electricity, and protect communities from climate change.

As temperatures rise, precipitation patterns change, and extreme weather events occur, climate change is putting more and more strain on energy systems. AI offers the insight and intelligence required to modify energy operations and infrastructures to meet these problems.

9.1. How AI Improves Power Outage Disaster Response

When wildfires, hurricanes, or other extreme events endanger power networks, artificial intelligence (AI) can significantly increase the speed and effectiveness of disaster response:

- **Predictive Outage Modelling:** To determine which areas are most vulnerable to outages, machine learning models examine past weather data, vegetation trends, and grid topology.

Example: AI-based models can identify transmission lines that are most likely to break during wildfires in California, enabling proactive shutdowns to avert larger fires.

- **Real-Time Incident Detection:** Drones and sensors driven by AI identify damage right after storms, speeding up response times.
    - **Case Study:** AI-powered drone surveys allowed for quicker mapping of damaged infrastructure and downed wires following Hurricane Ida, which resulted in a 30% quicker repair.
- **Resource Optimization**: Based on real-time damage assessments and the prioritizing of vital facilities, AI systems are able to autonomously deploy staff and distribute backup generation.
- **AI-Powered Power Outage Disaster Response**: Disasters caused by climate change, like hurricanes, floods, and wildfires, pose serious threats to energy infrastructure. In order to prevent downtime, safeguard vital infrastructure, and save lives, artificial intelligence (AI) is being used more and more to predict, identify, and react to such situations.

9.2. Predictive Outage Modelling

Before a calamity strikes, machine learning and artificial intelligence models can predict which areas are most vulnerable to power disruptions. These models find weaknesses in the transmission and distribution network by examining past weather trends, vegetation density, topography, soil moisture, and grid layout:

- **How It Operates:** AI algorithms generate probabilistic risk maps for power lines and substations by combining satellite imagery, weather predictions, and historical outage data.
- **Advantages:** Utilities can decrease the ignition of wildfires, plan for emergency resource allocation, and avert catastrophic failures by proactively shutting down lines in high-risk locations.
- **Example:** AI-based predictive models examined which transmission lines were most vulnerable to failure because of surrounding vegetation or strong winds during the California wildfires. Pre-emptive line shutdowns by utilities could stop major fires and lessen the harm to nearby neighbourhoods.

9.3. Real-Time Incident Identification

After hurricanes or other calamities, damage to energy infrastructure may be detected almost instantly thanks to AI-powered sensors, drones, and smart meters. Compared to conventional techniques, these solutions allow operators to prioritize recovery operations and determine the scope of outages considerably more quickly:

- **How it works:** To record structural damage, downed lines, and restricted access routes, drones fitted with LiDAR sensors and high-resolution cameras fly over the impacted locations. Real-time AI analysis of these photos identifies serious flaws.
- **Advantages**: Quick damage evaluation enables prompt response, minimizing downtime and averting secondary risks.
- **Case Study:** Drone surveys powered by AI were used to map thousands of miles of damaged infrastructure during Hurricane Ida in 2021. Compared to traditional evaluation techniques, the AI approach expedited restoration by 30% by automatically prioritizing high-risk regions for repair.

9.4. Resource Optimization

Based on real-time damage data and anticipated recovery times, artificial intelligence (AI) allows for the dynamic distribution of repair teams, emergency supplies, and backup power generation:

- **How It Operates**: AI systems provide optimal dispatch plans by combining outage forecasts, real-time sensor data, and logistical restrictions (e.g., equipment status, road access, and personnel availability).
- **Advantages**: As repair teams are effectively dispatched to restore wider service, vital institutions such as hospitals, water treatment facilities, and emergency shelters are guaranteed to receive electricity first.
- **Example:** AI can decide which substations should be restored first during wildfire or hurricane situations and which mobile generators should be brought out to ensure the continuation of critical services, thus lowering downtime and operating expenses.

AI Roadmap for Climate-Resilient Infrastructure

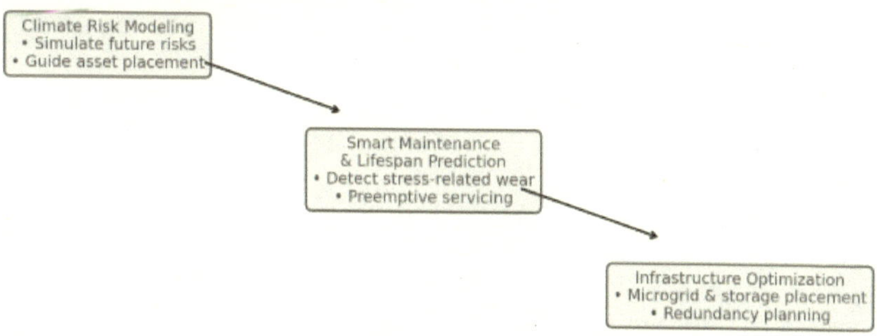

Figure 8: AI Roadmap for Climate-Resilient Infrastructure

Note: The above graphic roadmap demonstrates how AI helps build climate-resilient infrastructure:

- **Climate Risk modelling** → Vulnerabilities are identified and placement is guided by climate risk modelling.
- **Smart Maintenance & Lifespan Prediction** → Pre-emptive service helps avoid breakdowns.
- **Infrastructure optimization** → using storage and microgrids to provide redundancy and dependable power.

In conclusion, energy crisis management is transformed from reactive to proactive by the combination of AI-driven resource optimization, real-time problem identification, and predictive outage modelling. In addition to reducing service interruptions, artificial intelligence (AI) improves public safety and infrastructure resilience by foreseeing failures, identifying damage right once, and optimizing response.

9.5. Adaptive Techniques for Hydropower-Related Droughts

Hydropower is extremely dependent on the supply of water. AI supports dynamic resource management during drought:

- **Predictive Water Flow Modelling**: AI predicts water shortages and modifies turbine operations in response by combining weather forecasts, river flow statistics, and reservoir levels.
- **Optimal Energy Mix Coordination**: AI can preserve grid stability during droughts by boosting output from solar, wind, or thermal sources to make up for hydropower shortages.

Example: AI models have been used in the Western United States to maximize the combination of solar, wind, and hydropower during protracted droughts in order to avoid blackouts.

- **Demand Response Integration:** Demand-side management powered by AI can encourage lower energy use during times when hydropower is scarce, reducing system stress.

9.6. Using AI to Manage Hydropower Adaptively During Droughts

Hydropower is extremely dependent on the supply of water. Long-term droughts or erratic rainfall can lower reservoir levels, which would restrict the amount of power that can be generated and jeopardize the reliability of the grid. AI offers advanced methods to foresee, control, and lessen these difficulties.

9.6.1. Predictive Water Flow Modelling

AI predicts water availability and maximizes hydropower operations by utilizing machine learning and data analytics:

- **How It Works:** To estimate water inflows and possible shortages, AI models combine historical precipitation data, river flow measurements, snowpack levels, weather forecasts, and reservoir storage data.
- **Advantages:** To ensure steady electricity production, operators can take proactive measures like modifying turbine output, preserving water in reservoirs, or setting up alternate energy sources.
- **Example:** Predictive modelling can notify operators to lower turbine throughput ahead of time during dry spells, saving water for crucial times and preventing abrupt declines in hydropower output.

9.6.2. Optimal Energy Mix Coordination

By cleverly coordinating alternative renewable and conventional energy sources, artificial intelligence (AI) contributes to grid stability when hydropower output decreases:

- **How It Operates**: AI algorithms keep an eye on fossil fuel or thermal generation capacity, renewable output (wind, solar), and grid demand. AI suggests or automatically deploys complementary energy sources to balance supply based on anticipated hydropower shortages.
- **Advantages:** This cooperation guarantees a steady supply of energy even during droughts, avoids blackouts, and lessens dependency on pricey peaking plants.
- **Case Study:** During protracted droughts in the Western United States, AI models are utilized to dynamically modify the hydro, wind, and solar mix. In order to preserve dependability and lower carbon emissions, the system predicts hydropower shortages and boosts output from alternative renewable sources.

9.6.3. Integration of Demand Response

In order to reduce the strain on water-limited hydroelectric resources, AI also controls consumption patterns:

- **How It Operates:** Demand-side management platforms powered by AI examine consumption trends and apply load-shifting incentives, dynamic pricing, or automated energy-saving strategies for commercial, residential, and industrial customers.
- **Advantages:** AI guarantees that the available water is used effectively by lowering peak demand during low-hydropower periods, avoiding expensive imports from fossil-based generation and averting grid instability.
- **Example:** Amid drought-related shortages, utilities can

modify smart appliances or send targeted messages to cut down on energy consumption, thereby relieving pressure on hydroelectric reservoirs while preserving consumer comfort.

In conclusion, artificial intelligence (AI) revolutionizes hydropower management during droughts by facilitating intelligent demand-side management, dynamic energy source coordination, and proactive water flow forecasting. When combined, these tactics improve grid stability, maximize the integration of renewable energy sources, and reduce negative effects on the environment and the economy during times of water scarcity.

9.7. Using AI to Create Climate-Resilient Energy Systems

AI makes it possible to build and run infrastructure that is resistant to long-term climate stressors, going beyond urgent crisis response:

- **Climate Risk Modelling for Grid Design**: AI can model how future storms, flooding, and temperature extremes may affect infrastructure, directing the location of lines, substations, and renewable resources.
- **Smart Maintenance and Lifespan Prediction:** AI forecasts how climate stressors like heat, humidity, and salt corrosion will accelerate equipment deterioration, enabling preventative maintenance to avert failures.
- **Infrastructure Optimization**: To guarantee continuity in the face of adversity, machine learning algorithms optimize the location, storage capacity, and redundancy of microgrids.
- **Example:** In typhoon-prone areas of Japan, AI-optimized microgrids guarantee that vital infrastructure, such as hospitals, stays powered even during intense storms.

9.8. Using AI to Create Climate-Resilient Energy Systems

Energy infrastructure must be able to endure more frequent and severe weather events including heatwaves, floods, storms, and typhoons as climate change worsens. AI offers the intelligence to foresee dangers, optimize designs, and maintain vital systems, guaranteeing dependable energy delivery even in the most adverse circumstances.

9.8.1. **Climate Risk Modelling for Grid Design**: AI allows engineers and energy planners to model how climate change will affect energy infrastructure in the long run:

- **How It Operates**: In order to forecast the potential effects of temperature extremes, flooding, or storms on substations, transmission lines, and renewable installations, machine learning and simulation models analyse historical weather data, climate projections, topography information, and asset vulnerability assessments.
- **Advantages:** By arranging renewable energy sources for optimal dependability, strengthening lines in wind-prone locations, and locating assets away from high-risk flood zones, utilities may create resilient grids from the ground up.
- **Example:** AI can suggest raising important transformers or creating backup transmission lines in flood-prone areas to avoid outages during periods of intense precipitation.

9.8.2. **Lifespan Prediction and Intelligent Maintenance**

AI enables preventive maintenance by anticipating and reducing equipment deterioration brought on by climate stressors:

- **How It Operates**: To estimate equipment lifespan and detect components at risk of failure, AI models examine temperature variations, humidity levels, salt exposure, corrosion rates, and past failure data.
- **Advantages:** By planning maintenance before major malfunctions happen, utilities may prolong the life of valuable assets, cut down on downtime, and save repair expenses.
- **Example:** AI can identify when a substation transformer is vulnerable to insulation degradation brought on by heat, triggering preventive maintenance to prevent an outage during a heat wave.

9.8.3. **Optimization of Infrastructure**

Additionally, AI optimizes energy infrastructure placement, design, and redundancy to guarantee continuation in the face of adversity:

- **How It Operates**: In order to identify the most resilient design, machine learning algorithms analyse a variety of scenarios while balancing variables including energy demand, grid topology, the availability of renewable resources, storage capacity, and risk exposure.
- **Advantages:** Even in the event of grid failure, a continuous power supply is guaranteed by the strategic positioning of microgrids, batteries, and backup generators. Planning for redundancy lowers the chance of disruptions.
- **Example:** AI-optimized microgrids have been installed in typhoon-prone areas of Japan to ensure that vital infrastructure, such as hospitals, emergency rooms, and water treatment facilities, are powered during strong storms, protecting public health and safety.

In brief: AI turns energy infrastructure into dynamic, climate-aware networks instead of static, reactive systems. AI makes ensuring that grids are resilient, flexible, and able to continue providing critical services even in the face of severe environmental stress by using risk modelling, predictive maintenance, and optimum design.

9.8.4. **The following are important lessons learned:**

a. AI turns reactive catastrophe response into proactive and predictive management.
b. AI-driven adaptive tactics lessen the effects of climate-related fluctuations in renewable energy sources.
c. AI integration into energy infrastructure planning, design, and maintenance is essential for long-term climate resilience.

Chapter 10: Human Factor, Ethics, and Policy

10.1. The Difficulties of Regulating AI in Critical Infrastructure

Unprecedented efficiency, robustness, and predictive capacities are brought about by AI integration in energy systems, but it also presents difficult regulatory issues. Power grids, gas networks, and water systems are examples of critical infrastructure that is extremely sensitive; even small AI errors could result in widespread blackouts or cascading catastrophes.

Important difficulties include:

10.1.1. Certification and Standardization

Governments and international organizations are rushing to establish precise rules for artificial intelligence in vital infrastructure, which is still a frontier technology. Usually, these requirements include:

- **Reliability:** Making sure AI systems continuously function as planned in a variety of operational scenarios, including severe occurrences like storms or blackouts. For instance, artificial intelligence (AI) used to control a grid must continue to distribute energy even when demand increases unexpectedly.
- **Explainability:** Regulators require that AI judgments be comprehensible and transparent. The rationale for an AI system's prioritization of particular energy flows or the postponement of a maintenance notice must be explicable to utilities. This is particularly crucial for audits and post-event investigations.
- **Safety:** AI must not jeopardize cyber or physical security. An AI system in charge of substations, for example, ought to stop dangerous voltage swings and overloads.

Inconsistent use of AI technologies by utilities in the absence of uniform certification could result in disjointed safety procedures, incompatible systems, and possible susceptibilities to cyberattacks and technical malfunctions.

Example: Many nations still only require voluntary use of the IEEE P7000 series, which offers guidelines for safe and ethical AI design, especially in critical infrastructure.

10.1.2. Accountability and Liability

Accountability gets complicated legally when AI systems distribute energy automatically:

- **Shared Accountability**: The utility implementing the AI, the provider of the AI software, and the operators keeping an eye on the system are all parties engaged. In the event of a failure, each may be held partially accountable.
- **Regulatory Clarity:** When AI mistakes result in outages, equipment damage, or monetary loss, laws must outline who is legally liable. Without this clarity, utilities could be reluctant to implement AI widely, which would impede innovation.
- **Insurance and Risk Transfer**: Insurance is impacted by well-defined liability frameworks. AI-related failures must be covered by policies for AI vendors and utilities.

Example: if an AI causes a blackout by miscalculating load distribution during periods of high demand, authorities must decide if the issue is with the operator's error, the AI's algorithm, or both. Liability rules tailored to AI in high-risk industries are being developed in nations like Germany.

10.1.3. Management of Ethical Risk

Decisions made by AI in energy systems frequently have practical repercussions:

- **Fair Access:** An AI may ration energy when supplies are limited. Algorithms must be created to prevent socioeconomic bias or to give preference to industrial users over residential locations.
- **Transparency:** Regulators demand that utilities explain the ethical frameworks included into their AI and the criteria used to make decisions.
- **Algorithmic Bias Mitigation:** Constant observation guarantees AI doesn't inadvertently discriminate, for example, by giving lower-income communities less priority when it comes to energy distribution.

Example: When it was discovered that AI-controlled energy distribution in India gave preference to business districts over residential regions, smart grid pilots came under fire. A fairness audit was required by regulators prior to broader implementation.

10.1.4. Adaptation of Dynamic Policies

Because AI is developing so quickly, static regulatory measures are insufficient:

- **Constant Monitoring:** To keep an eye on AI-driven systems and identify irregularities, noncompliance, or bias almost instantly, regulators may use AI technologies themselves.
- **Adaptable Guidelines:** To stay up with new AI capabilities, new dangers, and cutting-edge grid technologies, policies

should permit iterative revisions.

- **Sandbox Settings:** Regulatory "sandboxes" reduce risk and promote innovation by enabling utilities to test AI technologies under supervision prior to full deployment.

Example: the Financial Conduct Authority (FCA) of the United Kingdom established regulatory sandboxes for fintech AI; electricity grids are considering adopting similar models to safely test AI in real-world scenarios.

This enlarged perspective highlights that AI in critical infrastructure is a legal, ethical, and regulatory concern rather than merely a technical one. Standards, accountability, equity, and flexibility must all be included into effective governance in order to preserve operational security and public confidence.

Case Example: The AI Act in the European Union aims to categorize high-risk AI applications, such as those in energy systems, and enforce stringent auditing and transparency standards to guarantee ethical compliance and safety.

10.2. Ownership and Data Privacy in Smart Energy Systems

Massive data flows from homes, businesses, and industrial activities are essential to predictive AI, smart grids, and IoT-enabled meters. This brings up important issues regarding ownership and privacy.

Among the factors are:

10.2.1. Consumer Control and Consent

Artificial intelligence (AI) in smart energy systems depends on detailed information from homes and businesses, such as appliance activity, energy usage trends, and occasionally even location or behavioural data. In order to preserve customer autonomy, utilities must:

- **Transparency:** Be transparent about the data they gather, why they collect it, how they plan to handle it, and who can access it. Terms of service that are unclear or complicated might erode confidence.
- **Consent Management**: Instead of being enrolled automatically, consumers should voluntarily consent to data acquisition. It should also be possible for them to withdraw their consent at any moment.
- **Data Anonymisation**: By anonymizing sensitive data prior to analysis, such as household occupancy patterns or appliance-level usage, privacy risk can be decreased while AI optimization is still possible.
- **Control Interfaces:** Customers should have dashboards to view, manage, and download their data from smart meters and energy apps.

Example: the **General Data Protection Regulation (GDPR)** in the EU imposes stringent guidelines on smart energy providers on user consent, necessitating easy access to personal data and unambiguous opt-in procedures.

10.2.2. Data Sovereignty

Cross-border AI applications may be complicated by local privacy and security rules that apply to data obtained within a nation:

- **National Authorities:** Local laws governing data processing, sharing, and storage must be followed. For example, even if a multinational energy firm processes data obtained in France, it still needs to adhere to French privacy rules.
- **Cross-Border Challenges**: Cloud-based grid management systems and regional AI energy trading platforms must concurrently traverse several legislative frameworks, frequently necessitating distinct data processing and storage solutions for each country.
- **Localization Requirements:** In order to safeguard its infrastructure and inhabitants' privacy, several nations require that energy data be stored on servers located within their boundaries.

Multinational grid AI deployments are impacted by China's stringent data localization regulations, which forbid energy businesses from storing domestic customer data on overseas servers without express consent.

10.2.3. Public Good vs. Commercial Use

The public interest must be weighed with the commercial benefit of energy usage data, which utilities might use to create operational insights, predictive services, or targeted marketing:

- **Risks of Monetization:** Selling user data in an opaque manner might erode confidence and break privacy regulations.
- **Regulatory Balance:** While preventing abuse, regulators must permit data-driven innovation that benefits society and consumers, such as enhancing grid efficiency or facilitating demand response initiatives.
- **Public Interest Projects:** Projects that improve accessibility, resilience, or sustainability may be given precedence over those that are just focused on profit under data sharing agreements.

Example: Certain utilities in the US collaborate with academic institutions to use anonymized smart meter data for energy efficiency research while forbidding the commercial transfer of personally identifiable customer information.

10.2.4. Risks of Security Breach

Energy networks' AI systems are particularly vulnerable to hacks since they manage both operational and personal data:

- **Operational Disruption**: A hack might interfere with AI-powered grid control, leading to equipment damage, cascading failures, or blackouts.
- **Risks to Consumer Privacy**: If an attacker were to obtain

detailed energy data, they could be able to deduce occupancy, household habits, or delicate lifestyle trends.

- **Cybersecurity Measures**: Both the AI models and the underlying data architecture need to use encryption, multi-factor authentication, and intrusion detection. Frequent penetration tests and audits are essential.
- **AI-Specific Threats:** Robust model monitoring and anomaly detection are necessary to prevent adversarial assaults on AI models, such as data poisoning or input manipulation, which can impair decision-making.

Example: The necessity for AI-aware security measures was highlighted in 2020 when a ransomware attack on the IT network of a US utility showed how cybersecurity breaches could jeopardize both operational management and customer data privacy.

These four domains collectively demonstrate how data in smart energy systems can be both a strength and a weakness. As important as AI algorithms themselves are safeguarding systems, preserving privacy, and upholding consumer rights.

For instance: Strict privacy regulations in California require utility providers to anonymize consumer data while allowing AI-driven grid optimization through smart meter initiatives.

10.3. Retraining Energy Workers for a Future Driven by AI

The energy workforce is *undergoing a significant transition as AI automates demand forecasting, predictive maintenance, and routine monitoring.* Conventional responsibilities in planning, maintenance, and operations need to change.

Important reskilling techniques include:

10.3.1. Up-Skilling Operators

Human operators must concentrate on *exception management and strategic oversight* as AI takes over increasingly repetitive monitoring and control duties in energy systems:

- **Interpreting AI Insights**: Operators need to become proficient in deciphering forecasts, alerts, and suggestions produced by AI. This involves identifying biases, abnormalities, or false positives in prediction models.
- **Real-Time Decision-Making**: In emergency situations like load shedding, grid rerouting, or fault response, operators would have to override AI judgments. Safer, quicker interventions are ensured when the reasoning behind AI recommendations is understood.
- **Scenario-Based Training**: By simulating demand surges, grid outages, or renewable intermittency, operators can practice reacting to atypical circumstances with AI assistance.

Example: smart grid operators in Germany receive AI-assisted control room training, where people manage unforeseen situations while AI forecasts direct decision-making.

10.3.2. Technical Training

To manage, maintain, and enhance AI systems, energy engineers and technical personnel need to pick up specific skills:

- **Competencies in AI and Machine Learning**: Engineers may efficiently audit AI systems by having a solid understanding of model building, hyper parameter tuning, and performance evaluation.
- **Proficiency in Data Analytics:** To guarantee system dependability, engineers must examine operational data, identify trends, and verify AI forecasts.
- **Governance and Ethics:** Certifications in cybersecurity, AI ethics, and regulatory compliance are becoming more and more important. Engineers are responsible for making sure AI choices comply with safety, ethical, and regulatory requirements.
- **Integration Skills**: Engineers can more easily implement AI tools when they have a solid understanding of cloud computing, IoT platforms, and smart grid architecture.

Example: Singapore Power provides engineers with specific training in AI model audits, critical infrastructure cybersecurity, and ethical AI deployment, allowing for the secure integration of demand forecasting and predictive maintenance solutions.

10.3.3. Human-AI Collaborative Teams

Though they can't completely replace human judgment, AI systems can improve decision-making. Collaboration between humans and AI should be emphasized in training programs:

- **Role Definition:** Efficiency is ensured by clearly defining the duties that humans and AI must perform. AI handles routine optimization and large-scale data processing, while humans make judgment-based decisions.
- **Accountability and Trust:** Employees must learn to have faith in AI results without becoming overly dependent on them. Validating AI recommendations and comprehending their limitations are key components of training.
- **Team Dynamics**: By simulating actual energy operations, collaboration exercises educate teams how to integrate operational knowledge with AI insights.

Example: National Grid engineers in the UK take part in hybrid operations simulations where operators make decisions in real time and AI forecasts load surges, improving efficiency and safety.

10.3.4. A Culture of Constant Learning

AI tools change quickly, therefore worker training can't stay the same. It is crucial to foster a culture of lifelong learning:

- **Micro-learning And Modular**: Staff members can refresh their knowledge of cybersecurity protocols, AI tools, and grid optimization strategies without interfering with business operations thanks to brief, targeted learning modules.
- **Adaptive Learning Platforms**: AI-driven learning programs monitor staff development, provide tailored courses, and

model changing business conditions.

- **Knowledge Sharing:** Peer-to-peer learning is promoted by internal forums, workshops, and cross-departmental projects, guaranteeing that collective intelligence develops in tandem with AI capabilities.
- **Ongoing Certification:** Staff members maintain their expertise when AI models, legal frameworks, and grid technologies change thanks to frequent refresher training and advanced certifications.

> **Example:** in order to stay up with the quickly changing AI-driven grid technology, Pacific Gas & Electric (PG&E) employs ongoing AI literacy programs for engineers and operators that combine online modules, scenario simulations, and workshops.

This strategy guarantees that even as AI changes the operating environment, the energy workforce will continue to be essential, flexible, and productive.

As an illustration, Singapore Power has put in place a workforce reskilling program that improves operational efficiency and safety by providing engineers and technicians with practical training in AI-driven predictive maintenance and grid optimization technologies.

Diagram: Reskilling the Energy Workforce for the AI Era

Skill Area	Focus	Training Approach	Example / Case Study
Up-skilling Operators	Equip control room and field operators to interpret AI-generated insights, focus on exception management, and make informed decisions when AI systems encounter anomalies.	- Simulation-based training for real-time grid events. - Workshops on interpreting AI dashboards and alerts. - Decision-making drills involving AI-human coordination.	**Germany:** Smart grid operators trained using AI simulation platforms to handle emergencies while maintaining oversight of automated systems.
Technical Training	Build deep technical competence in AI, machine learning, and data analytics to design, audit, and maintain intelligent energy systems.	- Specialized certification in AI model management and auditing. - Hands-on training in ML algorithms, cybersecurity, and ethical AI deployment. - Cross-disciplinary workshops blending IT and energy engineering.	**Singapore Power:** Engineers trained in AI model validation, ethical governance, and cyber-physical system security for predictive maintenance and load optimization.

Skill Area	Focus	Training Approach	Example / Case Study
Collaborative Human-AI Teams	Develop strong collaboration between human expertise and AI capabilities, ensuring balanced decision-making and trust in AI outcomes.	- Role-based training defining AI vs. human responsibilities. - Trust calibration workshops to prevent overreliance on AI. - Multi-role simulations for hybrid decision environments.	**UK National Grid:** Operators and AI systems jointly manage real-time demand response, with engineers trained to interpret AI predictions and act on anomalies.
Continuous Learning Culture	Foster a long-term learning mind-set where employees constantly update skills to keep pace with evolving AI tools and regulations.	- Modular and micro learning programs for ongoing skill refresh. - AI-driven learning platforms that recommend personalized content. - Internal knowledge-sharing communities	

Skill Area	Focus	Training Approach	Example / Case Study
		and periodic re-certifications.	

Figure 9: Reskilling the Energy Workforce for the AI Era

10.3.5. Important Takeaway:

Retraining the energy workforce is a deliberate shift, not a one-time endeavour. *Energy companies can guarantee that human expertise stays at the centre of AI-powered operations by including technical, ethical, and collaborative training.* This will promote resilience, accountability, and creativity in the age of digital energy.

In conclusion: The human element is highlighted as both a limitation and a facilitator at the nexus of AI, ethics, and policy in energy systems. Adaptive governance, strong privacy standards, and an empowered workforce that can navigate the AI-powered energy environment are all necessary for the effective implementation of AI, in addition to technical innovation. In this sense, people continue to play a crucial role in ensuring that AI enhances rather than diminishes societal and infrastructure resilience.

Chapter 11: The Future: Artificial Intelligence's Contribution to the Net-Zero Revolution

Overview

Policy incentives and the deployment of renewable energy will not be the only factors in the shift to a net-zero planet. As a revolutionary force, artificial intelligence (AI) is speeding up the transition to carbon neutrality, changing energy systems, and possibly establishing an internationally networked energy ecosystem.

11.1. Global Carbon Neutrality and AI: Promoting the Sustainable Development Goals (SDGs) of the United Nations

Numerous UN SDGs, including Goal 7 (Affordable and Clean Energy), Goal 9 (Industry, Innovation, and Infrastructure), Goal 11 (Sustainable Cities), and Goal 13 (Climate Action), are greatly aided by artificial intelligence (AI). Among its contributions are:

11.1.1. Carbon Monitoring and Prediction

A fundamental shift in how governments, municipalities, and businesses track and control emissions is represented by AI-driven carbon tracking. Conventional reporting techniques depend on manual data collection or recurring surveys, which are frequently unreliable, insufficient, or delayed. This is altered by AI, which combines several real-time data sources:

- **Satellite Imagery Analysis:** Methane leaks from oil and gas activities, rates of deforestation, and even the concentration of carbon dioxide over urban and industrial regions can all be detected using high-resolution satellite data. Large-scale processing of these photos by AI models allows them to spot patterns and abnormalities far more quickly than human analysts could.
- **Internet of Things Sensor Networks:** Emissions data is continuously reported by smart sensors installed in manufacturing facilities, power plants, and transportation networks. This data is compiled and analysed by AI algorithms, which provide a real-time, updateable carbon footprint map.

- **Predictive Hotspot Identification:** AI can predict areas where emissions are anticipated to increase, such as busy city areas or industrial clusters during periods of peak output, by using machine learning models on historical and real-time data. The impact can then be lessened by policymakers enacting targeted actions like short-term traffic restrictions, demand-side energy changes, or pollution fines.
- **Case Study:** To forecast city-level emissions trends in Singapore, AI-powered carbon mapping integrates building energy consumption, industrial output, and traffic data. High-emission neighbourhoods can be given priority by authorities for renewable integration or efficiency improvements.

11.1.2. Improving Manufacturing Procedures

The manufacturing of steel, cement, chemicals, and aluminium are examples of energy-intensive industries that contribute significantly to global greenhouse gas emissions. AI has two advantages: it lowers operating costs and emissions. Among the main methods are:

- **Production Scheduling Optimization**: AI algorithms modify the scheduling of production in accordance with cost, carbon intensity, and energy availability. For instance, reducing dependency on fossil fuels can be achieved by moving energy-intensive businesses to times when renewable energy is plentiful.
- **Predictive maintenance:** AI examines sensor data from equipment to find wear or inefficiency early on. Factories can avoid energy waste from unplanned downtime or malfunctioning equipment by anticipating breakdowns before they happen.
- **Process Efficiency Improvement:** Real-time optimization of

furnace temperatures, chemical mix ratios, and conveyor speeds by machine learning models guarantees that energy consumption is kept to a minimum without sacrificing output quality.

Example: An example of how intelligent operations and climate goals are directly related is provided by a European cement mill where AI-enabled predictive maintenance and process optimization decreased energy consumption by 18% and carbon emissions proportionately. Similarly, steel producers have achieved 15–20% energy savings when they use AI to optimize blast furnace operations.

11.1.3. Planning for Climate-Responsive Energy

Because solar energy depends on sunshine and wind energy depends on weather, renewable energy is by its very nature changeable. AI makes it possible for climate-resilient, adaptive energy planning that minimizes dependency on fossil fuels while balancing supply and demand:

- **Demand Forecasting:** To forecast energy demand at the local, regional, or national level, machine learning algorithms examine past consumption trends, weather predictions, and socioeconomic variables.
- **Renewable Supply Forecasting:** AI forecasts solar and wind power with a high degree of accuracy, taking seasonal and short-term weather fluctuations into consideration. As a result, less fossil fuel backup is required in an emergency.
- **Scenario-Based Planning:** In order to predict grid stress, utilities can model various climatic scenarios, such as heat waves, storms, and droughts. To preserve stability, AI suggests flexible loads, renewable dispatch, and the best possible

storage deployment.

- **Carbon-Aware Grid Operations:** AI can reduce overall emissions without sacrificing dependability by giving preference to low-carbon sources during periods of peak demand or when fossil fuel-heavy power is unavoidable.
- **Case Example:** Artificial intelligence (AI)-powered energy management systems in California plan energy storage and dispatch by predicting wind and solar output in addition to electricity demand. AI avoided outages and decreased dependency on natural gas peaker plants by coordinating battery usage and flexible loads during extreme heatwaves.

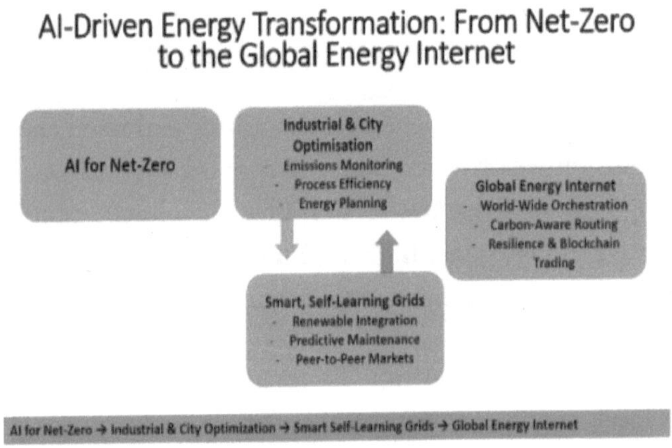

Figure 10: AI-Driven Energy Transformation: From Net-Zero to the Global Energy Internet

Note: The above **visual framework** shows the progression from **AI for Net-Zero → Industrial & City Optimization → Smart Self-Learning Grids → Global Energy Internet**.

In brief: These three pillars—industrial optimization, climate-responsive planning, and carbon tracking—showcase how AI turns net-zero goals from abstract objectives into workable, quantifiable plans. A feedback loop is produced by the combination of real-time data, predictive algorithms, and operational control. AI tracks emissions, plans energy flows, and optimizes operations, all of which hasten the transition to a carbon-neutral future.

Through these uses, artificial intelligence (AI) unites sustainability and technical progress, turning global carbon neutrality into an attainable goal rather than an ideal.

11.2. Smart Grid Development into Decentralized, Self-Learning Ecosystems

Conventional grids are changing into intelligent, dynamic networks with resilience and self-optimization capabilities:

11.2.1. Dispersion

Large regions are supplied by a few major power plants in the old electrical system, which is centralized. This approach is being transformed by AI into a decentralized network with locally optimized and distributed power generation:

- **Integration of Distributed Energy Resources (DERs):** Energy storage devices, community microgrids, rooftop solar panels, and small wind turbines are now all actively contributing to the grid. These various sources are coordinated by AI algorithms to keep the supply of electricity steady and balanced.
- **Autonomous Supply-Demand Balancing**: AI continuously tracks patterns of generation and consumption throughout the network, eliminating dependency on distant power plants and delivering energy from nearby sources as needed.
- **Cutting Transmission Losses:** Decentralized systems reduce the distance that electricity must travel, which lowers losses and boosts efficiency, by giving local energy usage priority.
- **Improving Resilience:** Localized energy systems are more resistant to major disturbances by nature. AI is capable of isolating disruptions, redirecting energy, and preserving service in the event of severe weather or equipment malfunctions.

Example: AI-powered microgrids in Germany balance local demand with rooftop solar output, lowering reliance on centralized coal plants and enhancing resilience at the neighbourhood level.

11.2.2. Self-Learning Systems

Grids can now continuously optimize and adapt thanks to AI, surpassing static control systems:

- **Continuous Learning from Operational Data:** To find patterns and maximize energy flow, AI models absorb historical trends, real-time sensor readings, and environmental data.
- **Reinforcement Learning for Dynamic Adaptation:** AI can make decisions in unpredictable situations thanks to reinforcement learning. For instance, AI can immediately boost battery discharge or send wind energy to preserve grid stability when solar output suddenly lowers.
- **Outage Prevention and Congestion Management:** AI keeps the grid stable even during periods of high demand by anticipating possible overloads and rerouting electricity to avoid cascade failures.

Case Study: In order to reduce traffic and avoid blackouts during heat waves, artificial intelligence (AI) technologies in California's grid modify the flow of solar, wind, and hydroelectric power every few seconds.

11.2.3. Predictive Upkeep and Dependability

Artificial intelligence (AI)-powered digital twins are digital copies of real grid infrastructure that allow for proactive maintenance and monitoring:

- **Simulating Failure Scenarios:** By modelling transformers, substations, transmission lines, and dispersed assets, digital twins may simulate failure scenarios and forecast how equipment will react to stress or severe weather.
- **Proactive Intervention Prescription:** AI uses digital twin simulations to suggest replacements, load modifications, or maintenance before breakdowns happen, cutting downtime and increasing asset lifespans.
- **Optimizing Maintenance Costs:** By using predictive insights, utilities can minimize operational expenses and prevent needless service outages by only doing maintenance when necessary.

Example: High-voltage substations in Japan include AI-driven digital twins that predict transformer problems months in advance, enabling personnel to repair parts proactively and avert blackouts.

11.2.4. Peer-to-Peer Energy Markets

At the local level, AI is making decentralized, market-driven energy trade possible:

- **Handling Energy Transactions:** Prosumers, or homes or businesses that generate and utilize energy, have the option to sell extra electricity to nearby residents or the community. AI uses pricing, supply, and demand to match buyers and sellers in real time.
- **Dynamic Pricing Based on Carbon Intensity:** AI algorithms take into account the carbon footprint of energy sources, restricting the use of fossil fuels during peak hours and encouraging usage when renewable supply is strong.
- **Enhancing Local Energy Autonomy:** Communities become

partially self-sufficient, relying less on distant, centralized power facilities. Additionally, this makes people more resilient to disturbances.

> **Example:** AI-managed peer-to-peer energy trading platforms in Brooklyn, New York, enable solar-equipped apartment complexes to sell extra energy to nearby structures, maximizing local usage and lowering dependency on the main grid.

In brief: AI turns the conventional grid into a robust, flexible, and carbon-conscious ecosystem by decentralizing generation, enabling self-learning optimization, putting predictive maintenance into practice, and establishing local energy markets. In addition to improving efficiency, these developments enable utilities and communities to take an active role in reaching net-zero energy targets.

An energy network that is self-healing, adaptive, and constantly learning is promised by the combination of AI and decentralized infrastructure.

11.3. A Forward-Looking Perspective: Is AI Able to Establish a Global Energy Internet?

An AI-powered global energy network that is genuinely integrated and allows for smooth cross-border transmission, trading, and optimization of energy might be the next big thing:

11.3.1. Orchestration of Global Energy

A disjointed energy landscape could be transformed into a coordinated, intelligent network by using AI to coordinate energy resources on a global scale:

- **Coordinated Renewable Generation:** AI systems may dynamically distribute electricity where it is most required by managing hydro reservoirs in South America, wind turbines in Europe, geothermal plants in Iceland, and solar farms in the Sahara.
- **Real-Time Energy Flow Management**: AI can instantly identify the best energy path for each location by examining demand trends, weather predictions, storage capacities, and transmission limitations.
- **Load Balancing across Continents:** Through intercontinental transmission infrastructure, energy surpluses in one region (such as Africa's midday solar peak) might be routed to shortage regions (such as Europe's night-time demand).
- **Integration with Local Grids:** AI would work in unison with both local and national grids, guaranteeing stability and reducing the demand for backup power produced using fossil fuels.

An example of a scenario: Imagine a heat wave with heavy demand for air conditioning in Europe. Sahara solar farms are producing at their highest level at the same time. AI might store extra solar energy for later use in batteries or hydrogen electrolysers while directing it to European grids.

11.3.2. Energy Routing That Considers Carbon

AI can optimize global electricity flows to reduce emissions by making energy decisions based on carbon impact:

- **Giving Low-Carbon Sources Priority:** When rerouting energy worldwide, the system would give preference to wind, solar, hydro, and nuclear over coal or gas.
- **Dynamic Carbon Pricing Integration:** AI could modify energy flows to areas where low-carbon alternatives are more urgent or cost-effective by combining market signals and carbon intensity data.
- **Reducing Regional Fossil Dependence:** Low-carbon regions might provide excess renewable energy to countries with carbon-heavy grids, reducing their dependency on fossil fuels without sacrificing dependability.

Example: In order to reduce total emissions and coal consumption, renewable energy imported from solar-rich Middle Eastern regions might be added to India's coal-heavy system during the winter months.

11.3.3. Adaptability to Severe Circumstances

In the case of extreme events and natural disasters, a worldwide network driven by AI might greatly increase the resilience of the energy system:

- **Instantaneous Rerouting:** AI can move power from unaffected locations to vital areas in the event that a hurricane damages a piece of the national grid, avoiding blackouts in data centres, hospitals, and emergency services.
- **Predictive Risk Management:** AI predicts grid stress points by utilizing historical event data and climate modelling, allowing for proactive modifications to transmission and storage flows.
- **Redundancy Coordination:** The network guarantees continuous service even in the event of severe weather or geopolitical disturbances by preserving several possible energy pathways.

Example Scenario: AI keeps vital services running after severe flooding in Southeast Asia by rerouting electricity from nearby, unaffected grids and maximizing renewable storage reserves.

11.4. Smart Contracts and Blockchain

The network would incorporate smart contracts and blockchain technology to function safely and openly on a global basis:

- **Decentralized, Secure Transactions**: Blockchain makes guarantee that energy exchanges between nations, towns, or communities are auditable and impenetrable.
- **Automated Smart Contracts**: When supply, demand, and carbon intensity conditions are satisfied, AI might carry out energy transactions automatically, guaranteeing equitable price and effective distribution.
- **Transparency and Trust:** All parties involved, from local prosumers to national utilities, have access to information about energy flow, pricing, and carbon impact, which lowers conflict and improves responsibility.
- **Facilitating International Energy Markets:** This technology may serve as the foundation for an international energy market where excess renewable energy is exchanged in almost real-time across national boundaries.

Example Scenario: Using blockchain-enabled smart contracts, a hydro plant in South America might automatically sell extra energy to industrial zones in Europe. Payments, delivery confirmation, and carbon credit accounting would all be carried out automatically.

In brief: Real-time orchestration, carbon-aware routing, robust operations, and secure decentralized transactions are all combined in a worldwide AI energy network. A world where energy flows intelligently across borders, emissions are kept to a minimum, and systems are resilient to climate threats is the future of energy management, despite its ambitious nature.

AI offers the computational intelligence, predictive foresight, and operational coordination required to make the vision of a global energy internet a reality in the ensuing decades, despite the technical, political, and regulatory obstacles that stand in its way.

Important Takeaways:

a. AI Accelerates the World's Net-Zero Objectives

Decarbonisation is *accelerated by artificial intelligence*, which is changing how utilities, businesses, and governments achieve net-zero goals:

- **Reducing Emissions:** AI continuously tracks carbon emissions from industry, cities, and transit systems. It enables targeted interventions that directly lower greenhouse gas emissions by locating emissions hotspots and forecasting spikes.
- **Efficiency of Industry:** AI schedules energy-intensive operations at times of renewable energy availability, optimizes production processes, and anticipates equipment failure to prevent inefficiencies in energy-intensive industries like steel, cement, and chemicals. This lowers operating expenses in addition to emissions.
- **Energy Planning:** To balance supply and demand in real-time, machine learning algorithms combine data from renewable generation, historical consumption trends, and weather forecasts. AI can predict when energy will be plentiful or scarce, allowing utilities to store extra energy,

move loads, or send out low-carbon substitutes.

- **Policy Support and Decision-Making:** Governments and regulators can prioritize infrastructure investments, create carbon pricing plans, or put into effect cost-effective and significant climate mitigation initiatives by using AI-generated insights.
- **Example:** AI systems in Singapore and a number of European towns combine building energy consumption, industrial output, and transportation data to forecast city-level emissions, allowing for focused efficiency improvements and carbon reductions.

a. Smart Grids as Self-Learning, Autonomous Networks

The *conventional, centralized grid is changing into an intelligent, dynamic ecosystem that can adapt and learn on its own*:

- **Smooth Integration of Renewables:** AI controls distributed energy resources (DERs), such as wind farms, rooftop solar, and battery storage, minimizing transmission losses and balancing local generation and consumption.
- **Continuous Learning:** To optimize energy flow and avoid interruptions, self-learning AI models adjust in real time to variations in weather patterns, electricity demand, and renewable output. Grids can dynamically anticipate and react to stress locations thanks to reinforcement learning.
- **Predictive Maintenance:** By simulating failure scenarios and recommending preventive actions, AI-driven digital twins of grid infrastructure increase equipment lifespan and save downtime.
- **Peer-to-peer Energy Markets:** AI dynamically modifies pricing and routing to match demand while giving preference

to low-carbon energy, allowing communities and prosumers to exchange excess energy locally through smart grids.

- **Impact:** By enhancing efficiency and resilience, these networks lessen dependency on fossil fuels and enable local communities to take an active role in energy management.

a. The Internet of Global Energy

A planetary-scale, AI-coordinated network known as the "*Global Energy Internet*" is a revolutionary next step in energy management:

- **Global Energy Coordination**: AI coordinates hydro reservoirs, wind turbines, solar farms, and storage systems across continents, guiding energy flows in real-time to the most critical locations.
- **Carbon-Aware Routing**: By prioritizing energy according to carbon intensity, low-carbon sources are sent out first, minimizing dependency on grids that rely heavily on fossil fuels.
- **Resilience and Disaster Response**: In the event of severe weather, earthquakes, or infrastructure failures, the network instantly reroutes power to ensure that vital services continue.
- **Secure Blockchain Transactions**: Smart contracts make it possible for transparent, real-time energy trade across countries, cities, and local communities, guaranteeing carbon accounting and equitable distribution.
- **Cross-Border Cooperation:** By allowing excess renewable energy from one area to balance out shortages in another, such a system promotes international energy cooperation and lowers emissions worldwide.

Example Vision: An intelligent, carbon-aware, and resilient global network coordinated by AI could provide excess electricity to Europe during the day from Sahara solar farms, while South American hydro storage fills in the gaps during periods of low wind in Asia.

In conclusion: The net-zero revolution is propelled by artificial intelligence (AI), which optimizes emissions, industrial processes, and energy planning; turns smart grids into self-learning, autonomous ecosystems; and creates the possibility of a daring, globally interconnected, carbon-conscious energy network. When taken as a whole, these developments reshape the energy landscape and increase the likelihood of a net-zero, resilient, and sustainable world.

Essentially, *AI is a strategic partner in humanity's quest for a connected, carbon-neutral energy future rather than merely a tool.*

Appendix: AI and Energy Glossary

Category 1: Artificial Intelligence & Data Science

No.	Term / Acronym	Meaning / Definition
1	**AI**	**Artificial Intelligence** — Machines performing tasks that normally require human intelligence.
2	**ML**	**Machine Learning** — Algorithms that learn from data to predict or optimize energy systems.
3	**DL**	**Deep Learning** — Advanced ML using multi-layer neural networks for complex pattern recognition.
4	**ANN**	**Artificial Neural Network** — Model inspired by the brain, used for forecasting demand or faults.
5	**DNN**	**Deep Neural Network** — Neural model with multiple layers for advanced analysis.
6	**RNN**	**Recurrent Neural Network** — Used for sequential data such as hourly or daily energy demand.
7	**LSTM**	**Long Short-Term Memory** — A type of RNN handling long-term dependencies in time-series data.
8	**CNN**	**Convolutional Neural Network** — For image-based analysis, such as solar panel defect detection.
9	**GAN**	**Generative Adversarial Network** — Generates synthetic data to improve training or simulations.
10	**NLP**	**Natural Language Processing** — AI that reads and interprets human language (e.g., maintenance reports).
11	**MLOps**	**Machine Learning Operations** — Framework for managing and deploying AI models in production.
12	**Anomaly Detection**	AI process identifying irregularities in data that may signal faults or inefficiencies.
13	**Predictive**	AI predicting equipment failures to schedule

No.	Term / Acronym	Meaning / Definition
	Maintenance	repairs before breakdowns.
14	Energy Forecasting	AI predicting future demand, generation, and prices using historical data.

Category 2: Internet of Things (IoT) & Smart Systems

No.	Term / Acronym	Meaning / Definition
15	**IoT**	**Internet of Things** — Network of connected devices collecting and transmitting energy data.
16	**IIoT**	**Industrial Internet of Things** — IoT used in industrial energy systems for real-time monitoring.
17	**AIoT**	**Artificial Intelligence of Things** — Integration of AI with IoT for autonomous decision-making.
18	**Edge Computing**	Processing data locally at the device level for faster, low-latency decision-making.
19	**Cloud Computing**	Centralized processing and storage of massive energy datasets for AI analytics.
20	**Big Data**	Extremely large datasets analysed by AI to detect patterns and trends.
21	**Data Lake**	Central repository for structured and unstructured energy data used in AI training.
22	**FDD**	**Fault Detection and Diagnostics** — AI identifying faults in equipment through sensor data.
23	**SLP**	**Smart Load Prediction** — Predicting consumer energy usage using IoT and AI insights.

Category 3: Energy Infrastructure & Grid Intelligence

No.	Term / Acronym	Meaning / Definition
24	**SCADA**	**Supervisory Control and Data Acquisition** — Monitors and controls grid operations in real time.
25	**EMS**	**Energy Management System** — AI platform optimizing consumption and generation.
26	**BEMS**	**Building Energy Management System** — Controls energy use in commercial or residential buildings.
27	**DER**	**Distributed Energy Resources** — Decentralized power sources like solar, wind, and storage.
28	**DR**	**Demand Response** — Adjusting power demand to balance grid load dynamically.
29	**DSM**	**Demand Side Management** — Managing consumer energy use for efficiency.
30	**VPP**	**Virtual Power Plant** — AI aggregation of distributed energy units acting as one power source.
31	**PMU**	**Phasor Measurement Unit** — Measures grid electrical waves for real-time stability analysis.
32	**GIS**	**Geographic Information System** — Maps and analyses spatial data for energy planning.
33	**Grid Optimization**	AI process balancing generation, storage, and consumption across networks.
34	**Smart Grid**	Intelligent, interconnected grid integrating AI, IoT, and automation.
35	**Microgrid**	Localized grid that can function independently or alongside the main grid.

Category 4: Renewable Energy & Sustainability

No.	Term / Acronym	Meaning / Definition
36	**RES**	**Renewable Energy Sources** — Solar, wind, hydro, and biomass power systems.
37	**PV**	**Photovoltaic** — Technology converting sunlight directly into electricity.
38	**CSP**	**Concentrated Solar Power** — Uses mirrors to concentrate sunlight for heat-based power generation.
39	**REMS**	**Renewable Energy Management System** — AI platform managing variable renewable generation.
40	**EV**	**Electric Vehicle** — Vehicle powered by batteries integrated with AI charging systems.
41	**V2G**	**Vehicle-to-Grid** — Technology allowing EVs to feed energy back to the grid.
42	**Carbon Footprint Monitoring**	AI tracking and reducing greenhouse gas emissions from energy systems.

Category 5: Operations, Analytics & Business Intelligence

No.	Term / Acronym	Meaning / Definition
43	**KPI**	**Key Performance Indicator** — Metrics measuring efficiency and performance of energy operations.
44	**O&M**	**Operations and Maintenance** — Routine management and upkeep of energy assets.
45	**CBM**	**Condition-Based Maintenance** — Maintenance based on real-time AI sensor data.
46	**Energy Analytics**	Using AI to interpret and visualize consumption, production, and cost data.
47	**P2P Energy Trading**	**Peer-to-Peer Energy Trading** — Decentralized trading of power between consumers via AI and blockchain.
48	**API**	**Application Programming Interface** — Software interface connecting AI applications to energy systems.
49	**VPP Forecasting**	Predictive AI modelling of **Virtual Power Plant** performance.
50	**Digital Twin**	Virtual AI replica of a physical energy system for simulation and optimization.

Table of Figures

Bibliography

1. *Azhar, Azeem (28 December 2024). "The 19th-Century Technology That Threatens A.I."[1] The New York Times.*

2. *"Explained: Generative AI's environmental impact"[2]. MIT News | Massachusetts Institute of Technology. 17 January 2025. Retrieved 14 July 2025.*

3. *Berreby, David (6 February 2024). "As Use of A.I. Soars, So Does the Energy and Water It Requires"[3]. Yale E360. Archived[4] from the original on 1 July 2024. Retrieved 14 July 2025.*

4. *Erdenesanaa, Delger (10 October 2023). "A.I. Could Soon Need as Much Electricity as an Entire Country"[5]. The New York Times. ISSN[6] 0362-4331[7]. Archived[8] from the original on 26 June 2024. Retrieved 14 July 2025.*

5. *Zhuk, A. (15 December 2023). "Artificial Intelligence Impact on the Environment: Hidden Ecological Costs and*

1. *https://www.nytimes.com/2024/12/28/opinion/ai-electricity-power-plants.html?searchResultPosition=8*
2. *https://news.mit.edu/2025/explained-generative-ai-environmental-impact-0117*
3. *https://e360.yale.edu/features/artificial-intelligence-climate-energy-emissions*
4. *https://web.archive.org/web/20240701032416/https:/e360.yale.edu/features/artificial-intelligence-climate-energy-emissions*
5. *https://www.nytimes.com/2023/10/10/climate/ai-could-soon-need-as-much-electricity-as-an-entire-country.html*
6. *https://en.wikipedia.org/wiki/ISSN_(identifier)*
7. *https://search.worldcat.org/issn/0362-4331*
8. *https://web.archive.org/web/20240626094901/https:/www.nytimes.com/2023/10/10/climate/ai-could-soon-need-as-much-electricity-as-an-entire-country.html*

Ethical-Legal Issues"[9]*. Journal of Digital Technologies and Law. 1 (4): 932–954. doi*[10]*:10.21202/jdtl.2023.40*[11]*. hdl*[12]*:10230/59428*[13]*. ISSN*[14] *2949-2483*[15]*. Archived*[16] *from the original on 6 July 2024. Retrieved 15 July 2025.*

6. *Hao, Karen (1 March 2024). "AI Is Taking Water From the Desert"*[17]*. The Atlantic. Archived*[18] *from the original on 6 July 2024. Retrieved 14 July 2025.*

7. *Macknick, Jordan; Newmark, Robin; Heath, Garvin; Hallett, K. (1 March 2011). Review of Operational Water Consumption and Withdrawal Factors for Electricity Generating Technologies*[19] *(Report). National Renewable Energy Laboratory. doi*[20]*:10.2172/1009674*[21]*. NREL/TP-6A20-50900.*

8. *Desislavov, Radosvet; Martínez-Plumed, Fernando; Hernández-Orallo, José (1 April 2023). "Trends in AI*

9. *https://www.lawjournal.digital/jour/article/view/303*

10. *https://en.wikipedia.org/wiki/Doi_(identifier)*

11. *https://doi.org/10.21202%2Fjdtl.2023.40*

12. *https://en.wikipedia.org/wiki/Hdl_(identifier)*

13. *https://hdl.handle.net/10230%2F59428*

14. *https://en.wikipedia.org/wiki/ISSN_(identifier)*

15. *https://search.worldcat.org/issn/2949-2483*

16. *https://web.archive.org/web/20240706180411/https:/www.lawjournal.digital/jour/article/view/303*

17. *https://www.theatlantic.com/technology/archive/2024/03/ai-water-climate-microsoft/677602/*

18. *https://web.archive.org/web/20240706180407/https:/www.theatlantic.com/technology/archive/2024/03/ai-water-climate-microsoft/677602/*

19. *https://doi.org/10.2172/1009674*

20. *https://en.wikipedia.org/wiki/Doi_(identifier)*

21. *https://doi.org/10.2172%2F1009674*

inference energy consumption: Beyond the performance-vs-parameter laws of deep learning"[22]. Sustainable Computing: Informatics and Systems. 38 100857. arXiv[23]:2109.05472[24]. Bibcode[25]:2023SCIS...3800857D[26]. doi[27]:10.1016/j.suscom.2023.100857[28]. ISSN[29] 2210-5379[30]. Archived[31] from the original on 23 June 2024. Retrieved 14 July 2025.

9. *Kolbert, Elizabeth (9 March 2024). "The Obscene Energy Demands of A.I."[32] The New Yorker. ISSN[33] 0028-792X[34]. Archived[35] from the original on 3 July 2024. Retrieved 15 July 2025.*

10. *Saenko, Kate (25 May 2023). "A Computer Scientist Breaks Down Generative AI's Hefty Carbon Footprint"[36].*

---

22. *https://www.sciencedirect.com/science/article/pii/S2210537923000124*
23. *https://en.wikipedia.org/wiki/ArXiv_(identifier)*
24. *https://arxiv.org/abs/2109.05472*
25. *https://en.wikipedia.org/wiki/Bibcode_(identifier)*
26. *https://ui.adsabs.harvard.edu/abs/2023SCIS...3800857D*
27. *https://en.wikipedia.org/wiki/Doi_(identifier)*
28. *https://doi.org/10.1016%2Fj.suscom.2023.100857*
29. *https://en.wikipedia.org/wiki/ISSN_(identifier)*
30. *https://search.worldcat.org/issn/2210-5379*
31. *https://web.archive.org/web/20240706180414/https:/www.sciencedirect.com/science/article/pii/S2210537923000124*
32. *https://www.newyorker.com/news/daily-comment/the-obscene-energy-demands-of-ai*
33. *https://en.wikipedia.org/wiki/ISSN_(identifier)*
34. *https://search.worldcat.org/issn/0028-792X*
35. *https://web.archive.org/web/20240703113448/https:/www.newyorker.com/news/daily-comment/the-obscene-energy-demands-of-ai*
36. *https://www.scientificamerican.com/article/a-computer-scientist-breaks-down-generative-ais-hefty-carbon-footprint/*

Scientific American. *Archived*[37] *from the original on 6 July 2024. Retrieved 14 July 2025.*

---

37. *https://web.archive.org/web/20240706180407/https:/www.scientificamerican.com/article/a-computer-scientist-breaks-down-generative-ais-hefty-carbon-footprint/*

Don't miss out!

Visit the website below and you can sign up to receive emails whenever Patrick Mukosha publishes a new book. There's no charge and no obligation.

https://books2read.com/r/B-A-HJNZ-MFLGH

BOOKS 2 READ

Connecting independent readers to independent writers.

Did you love *AI in Energy: Powering the Smart Grid*? Then you should read *AI in Education: Teaching the Machines to Teach*[38] by Patrick Mukosha!

[39]

AI in Education: Teaching the Machines to Teach

What happens when machines not only assist in learning but begin to *teach*? This ground-breaking book takes readers inside the rapidly evolving world of Artificial Intelligence in education, where algorithms are reshaping how knowledge is delivered, assessed, and personalized.

From classrooms equipped with adaptive tutoring systems to universities experimenting with automated grading and virtual teaching assistants, *AI in Education* reveals both the opportunities and the challenges of this transformation. Rich with real-world examples,

38. https://books2read.com/u/mgO10q

39. https://books2read.com/u/mgO10q

it shows how AI can help close learning gaps, empower students with disabilities, and support teachers in managing ever-growing workloads.

But this is not just a story of technological advancement—it is a human story. The book explores the irreplaceable role of educators as mentors, motivators, and ethical guides in an age when machines can replicate many cognitive tasks but not empathy, creativity, or moral judgment. It raises critical questions about equity, ethics, and the future of work for teachers and learners alike.

Accessible, insightful, and forward-looking, ***AI in Education: Teaching the Machines to Teach*** is an essential read for educators, policymakers, technologists, and parents who want to understand—and help shape—the future of learning in an AI-powered world.

"**Where human wisdom meets machine intelligence—the future of teaching begins.**" – Patrick Mukosha

Also by Patrick Mukosha

GoodMan

Resilient Strategies: Thriving in Harsh Business Conditions

Strategic Entrepreneurship: Navigating The Path To Success

Decisive Power: Navigating How to Make Toughest Decisions

"Reigning the Boardroom: A Trailblazing Guide to Corporate Governance Success"

Fortifying Digital Fortress: A Comprehensive Guide to Information Systems Security

“Unleashing the Power of Inclusive Innovation: Transforming the World for All”

“Exploring Computer Systems: From Fundamentals to Advanced Concepts”

“Computer Viruses Unveiled: Types, Trends and Mitigation Strategies”

"The Pinnacle of Success: Unveiling the World's 20 Most Successful Brands in 2023”

“Mastering Relational Databases: From Fundamentals to Advanced Concepts”

“Navigating Change: A Comprehensive Guide to Change Management”

“Information Systems Unraveled: Exploring the Core Concepts”

"Careers in Information Technology: Network Engineer"

“Careers in Information Technology: Network and Systems Administrator”
“Careers in Information Technology: Database Administrator”
"Careers in Information Technology: Cybersecurity Analyst"
“Careers in Information Technology: Cloud Security Specialist”
"Careers in Information Technology: Blockchain Developer"
"Careers in Information Technology: DevOps Engineer"
"Careers in Information Technology: Quality Assurance Analyst"
"Careers in Information Technology: Machine Learning Engineer"
"Careers in Information Technology: Artificial Intelligence (AI) Engineer"
"Careers in Information Technology: Internet of Things (IoT) Developer"
"Careers in Information Technology: AR/VR Developer"
“Careers in Information Technology: IoT Embedded Systems Designer”
“Careers in Information Technology: Artificial Intelligence (AI) Robotics Engineer”
“Careers in Information Technology: IoT Solutions Engineer”
“Careers in Information Technology: Data Scientist”
"Careers in Information Technology: Computer Vision Engineer"
"The Sociology of Information Technology"
“Smart Cities: The Technology Transforming Urban Living”
"The Future of Connectivity: Unleashing the Power of 5G and Beyond"
" Cybersecurity 2030 - Strategies for a Secure Digital Future"
The AI-Human Merger: Becoming Super-Intelligent Beings
AI Unleashed: The Future of Artificial Intelligence and Human Evolution
The Digital Prophet: Predicting the Next Decade of Disruption
AI in Agriculture: Farming the Future
AI in Education: Teaching the Machines to Teach

Deep Signal: AI and IoT Unlocking Underground Mining Communication

AI in Energy: Powering the Smart Grid

About the Author

Patrick Mukosha is an ICT & Management Consultant. With 15+ years of IT experience, he's passionate about all things ICT. He also loves to bring ICT down to a level that everyone can understand. His works have been quoted on Academia by Researchers and ICT Practitioners (www.academia.edu). He has a PHD and MBA from AIU, USA, BSc(Hons) ICT, UEA, UK, Dipl, CCT, UK. He's a founder of PatWest Technologies.

www.ingramcontent.com/pod-product-compliance
Lightning Source LLC
LaVergne TN
LVHW090356210926
848480LV00002B/353